Mushroom Recipes For Easy Everyday Meals

Arya .H King

All rights reserved. Copyright © 2024 Arya .H King

COPYRIGHT © 2024 Arya .H King

All rights reserved.

No part of this book must be reproduced, stored in a retrieval system, or shared by any means, electronic, mechanical, photocopying, recording, or otherwise, without written permission from the publisher.

Every precaution has been taken in the preparation of this book; still the publisher and author assume no responsibility for errors or omissions. Nor do they assume any liability for damages resulting from the use of the information contained herein.

Legal Notice:

This book is copyright protected and is only meant for your individual use. You are not allowed to amend, distribute, sell, use, quote or paraphrase any of its part without the written consent of the author or publisher.

Introduction

In the heart of every kitchen lies the potential for extraordinary culinary adventures, a sentiment vibrantly captured in this book.

This collection is more than a cookbook; it's a journey into the versatile world of mushrooms, an invitation to explore the depth of flavors and textures that these earthly treasures offer. From the robust and meaty Portobello to the delicate and slender Enoki, each mushroom variety brings its unique character to dishes, transforming the ordinary into the extraordinary.

Our odyssey begins with the majestic Portobello, a mushroom that commands attention not just for its size but for its rich, savory flavor that makes it a perfect meat substitute or a substantial addition to any dish. Imagine starting your culinary journey with a "25-Minute Tunisian Vegetable Couscous," where the Portobello adds a hearty depth, or the "Absolutely Fabulous Portobello Mushroom Tortellini," a dish that promises indulgence in every bite. The versatility of mushrooms is showcased through recipes that range from "All Day Venison Pot Roast" to "Zesty Grilled Portobello Mushrooms with Mashed Cannellini Beans and Harissa Sauce," each recipe a testament to the mushroom's ability to elevate a dish from the familiar to the memorable.

But this cookbook does more than offer recipes; it invites you to explore the myriad ways in which mushrooms can be incorporated into your daily meals. Whether it's the simplicity of a "Baked Asparagus with Portobello Mushrooms and Thyme" or the complexity of a "Beef Stew with Ale," where the mushrooms absorb and complement the ale's malty richness, there's a recipe for every occasion, taste, and skill level. The "Grilled Mushroom Sandwich With Citrus Mayo" stands as a beacon for those seeking a quick yet flavorful lunch option, while the "Portobello Mushroom Lentil Soup" offers comfort in a bowl, with the mushrooms imparting an umami-rich base that enriches the lentils.

As we delve deeper, the cookbook pays homage to the Enoki mushroom, a variety known for its delicate texture and mild, somewhat fruity flavor. The "ABC Ribeye Steak," crowned with Enoki mushrooms, presents a fusion of textures and flavors, where the tenderness of the steak meets the slight crunch of the Enoki. This section encourages you to explore the lighter, more nuanced side of mushrooms, with recipes designed to delight and surprise.

This book is more than a collection of recipes; it's a narrative that weaves through the seasons, celebrating the simplicity and complexity of mushrooms. It's an invitation to discover the joy of cooking with mushrooms, to experiment with new flavors, and to indulge in the comfort of familiar ones. Whether you're a seasoned chef or a curious novice, this cookbook offers something for everyone—a chance to explore, to taste, and to fall in love with mushrooms, one recipe at a time.

So, open your heart and your kitchen to the endless possibilities that mushrooms offer. Let this cookbook be your guide, a companion on a culinary journey that promises to be as enriching as it is delicious. Welcome to this book—where every day is an opportunity to discover the extraordinary in the ordinary, with mushrooms as your guide.

Contents

Chapter 1: Portobello 1
1. 25Minute Tunisian VegetableCouscous 2
   Ingredients 2
   Direction 3
   Nutrition Information 4
2. Absolutely Fabulous Portobello MushroomTortellini 5
   Ingredients 5
   Direction 6
   Nutrition Information 6
3. All Day Venison Pot Roast 7
   Ingredients 7
   Direction 8
   Nutrition Information 8
4. Asparagus and MushroomQuiche 9
   Ingredients 9
   Direction 9
   Nutrition Information 10
5. Asparagus Portobello Pasta 11
   Ingredients 11
   Direction 11
   Nutrition Information 12
6. Baked Asparagus with Portobello Mushrooms andThyme 13
   Ingredients 13
   Direction 13
   Nutrition Information 14
7. Baked Mushrooms andPotatoes with Spinach 15
   Ingredients 15
   Direction 15
   Nutrition Information 16
8. Baked Pasta with Sausageand Baby Portobello Mushroom White Sauce 17

Ingredients	17
Direction	17
Nutrition Information	18
9. Beef Stew with Ale	19
Ingredients	19
Direction	19
Nutrition Information	20
10. Beef Tenderloins with MushroomGarlic Sauce	21
Ingredients	21
Direction	21
Nutrition Information	22
11. Beths Portobello MushroomBurgers	23
Ingredients	23
Direction	23
Nutrition Information	24
12. Broccoli Rabe with PortobelloMushroom	25
Ingredients	25
Direction	25
Nutrition Information	26
13. Broccoli Salad with MargaritaDressing	27
Ingredients	27
Direction	27
Nutrition Information	28
14. Cabbage with PortobelloMushrooms	29
Ingredients	29
Direction	29
Nutrition Information	29
15. Cajun Chicken Pot Pie	31
Ingredients	31
Direction	31
Nutrition Information	32
16. Callys Omelet	33
Ingredients	33

Direction 33
Nutrition Information 33
17. Cannelloni Tre Sapori 35
Ingredients 35
Direction 35
Nutrition Information 36
18. Chardonnay ChickenSymphony 38
Ingredients 38
Direction 38
Nutrition Information 39
19. Chicken and PortobelloRollups 40
Ingredients 40
Direction 40
Nutrition Information 41
20. Chicken Artichoke and SpinachStuffed Portobellos 42
Ingredients 42
Direction 42
Nutrition Information 43
21. Chicken Marsala Florentine 44
Ingredients 44
Direction 44
Nutrition Information 45
22. Chicken Marsala with Portobello Mushrooms 46
Ingredients 46
Direction 46
Nutrition Information 47
23. Chicken With Portobello Mushrooms and Artichokes 48
Ingredients 48
Direction 48
Nutrition Information 49
24. ChineseStyle Baby Bok Choywith Mushroom Sauce 50
Ingredients 50
Direction 50

Nutrition Information 51
25. Couscous with Mushroomsand SunDried Tomatoes 52
Ingredients 52
Direction 52
Nutrition Information 53
26. Cream Cheese Alfredo Sauce 54
Ingredients 54
Direction 54
Nutrition Information 55
27. Creamy Beef Tips withMushrooms 56
Ingredients 56
Direction 56
Nutrition Information 57
28. Crock Pot Portobello Chicken 58
Ingredients 58
Direction 58
Nutrition Information 59
29. Easy Flat Iron Steak in WineSauce 60
Ingredients 60
Direction 60
Nutrition Information 61
30. Easy Mushroom Risotto withTrader Joes Cream of Mushroom Soup 62
Ingredients 62
Direction 62
Nutrition Information 63
31. Easy Portobello MushroomSaute 64
Ingredients 64
Direction 64
Nutrition Information 64
32. Exotic Mushroom and WalnutPate 66
Ingredients 66
Direction 66
Nutrition Information 67

33. Fettuccine Pasta withPortobello Mushrooms 68
Ingredients 68
Direction 68
Nutrition Information 69
34. Flat Iron Steak and SpinachSalad 70
Ingredients 70
Direction 70
Nutrition Information 71
35. Four Cheese Mashed Potato Stuffed Portobello Mushrooms 72
Ingredients 72
Direction 72
Nutrition Information 73
36. French Onion Mushroom GreenBeans 74
Ingredients 74
Direction 74
Nutrition Information 74
37. FrenchStyle Stuffed Portobellos with Green Beans 76
Ingredients 76
Direction 76
Nutrition Information 77
38. Giant Stuffed Mushrooms..78
Ingredients 78
Direction 78
Nutrition Information 79
39. Gourmet Cream Of WildMushroom Soup 80
Ingredients 80
Direction 80
Nutrition Information 81
40. Gourmet Gouda TurkeyBurgers 82
Ingredients 82
Direction 82
Nutrition Information 83
41. Great Grilled Smoky Vegetables with Avocado andGoat Cheese Crumbles 84

Ingredients 84
Direction 84
Nutrition Information 85
42. Green Bean and Portobello Mushroom Casserole 86
Ingredients 86
Direction 86
Nutrition Information 87
43. Grilled Chicken and Portobello Lasagna Rollups 88
Ingredients 88
Direction 88
Nutrition Information 89
44. Grilled Mushroom and Goat Cheese Rotini with Honey Garlic Chicken Kabobs 90
Ingredients 90
Direction 90
Nutrition Information 91
45. Grilled Mushroom Sandwich With Citrus Mayo 92
Ingredients 92
Direction 92
Nutrition Information 93
46. Grilled Portobello and Mozzarella 94
Ingredients 94
Direction 94
Nutrition Information 95
47. Grilled Portobello Mushrooms 96
Ingredients 96
Direction 96
Nutrition Information 96
48. Grilled Portobello Mushrooms with Blue Cheese 98
Ingredients 98
Direction 98
Nutrition Information 98
49. Grilled Portobello Mushrooms with Mashed Cannellini Beans and Harissa Sauce 100

Ingredients 100
Direction 101
Nutrition Information 101
50. Grilled Portobello Sandwich with Roasted Red Pepper and Mozzarella 103
Ingredients 103
Direction 103
Nutrition Information 104
51. Grilled Portobello with Basil Mayonnaise Sandwich 105
Ingredients 105
Direction 105
Nutrition Information 106
52. Grilled Portobellos Sauteed in Wine 107
Ingredients 107
Direction 107
Nutrition Information 108
53. Grilled Steak and Vegetable Salad from Publix 109
Ingredients 109
Direction 109
Nutrition Information 110
54. Grilled Stuffed Portobello Mushroom Caps 111
Ingredients 111
Direction 111
Nutrition Information 111
55. Grilled Tequila Portobello 113
Ingredients 113
Direction 113
Nutrition Information 113
56. Grilled Veggie Portobello Mushroom Burgers 115
Ingredients 115
Direction 115
Nutrition Information 116
57. Grilled Zucchini with Portobello and Goat Cheese 117
Ingredients 117

Direction 117

Nutrition Information 118

58. Grits a Ya Ya 119

Ingredients 119

Direction 119

Nutrition Information 120

59. Gunnar and Ravens BurgundySauce 121

Ingredients 121

Direction 121

Nutrition Information 122

60. Hot and Sour Tofu Soup SuanLa Dofu Tang 123

Ingredients 123

Direction 123

Nutrition Information 124

61. Hot Portobello MushroomSandwich 125

Ingredients 125

Direction 125

Nutrition Information 125

62. HummusStuffed PortobelloCaps 127

Ingredients 127

Direction 127

Nutrition Information 128

63. Individual Grilled VeggiePizzas 129

Ingredients 129

Direction 129

Nutrition Information 130

64. Instant Pot Bison Pasta PastaBisonte 131

Ingredients 131

Direction 131

Nutrition Information 132

65. Instant Pot Butternut SquashRisotto with Mushrooms 133

Ingredients 133

Direction 133

Nutrition Information 134

66. Jims BeerBattered PortobelloMushrooms 135
Ingredients 135
Direction 135
Nutrition Information 135

67. Kapusta 137
Ingredients 137
Direction 137
Nutrition Information 138

68. Kickin Portobello Dressing 139
Ingredients 139
Direction 139
Nutrition Information 140

69. Kohlrabi Kale Mushroom andBean Saute 141
Ingredients 141
Direction 141
Nutrition Information 142

70. Leek Potato MushroomCheddar Soup..143
Ingredients 143
Direction 143
Nutrition Information 144

71. Linguine with Clam Sauce andBaby Portobello Mushrooms...................................145
Ingredients 145
Direction 145
Nutrition Information 146

72. Linguine with PortobelloMushrooms..147
Ingredients 147
Direction 147
Nutrition Information 148

73. Mamitas Mojito Scallop Kabobs with Stuffed Tomatoes 149
Ingredients 149
Direction 150
Nutrition Information 150

74.	Marinated PortobelloMushrooms	152
	Ingredients	152
	Direction	152
	Nutrition Information	152
75.	Meatless Mushroom Tart	154
	Ingredients	154
	Direction	154
	Nutrition Information	155
76.	Megans Marvelous Mushrooms	156
	Ingredients	156
	Direction	156
	Nutrition Information	156
77.	Mushroom and OnionVegetarian Tacos	158
	Ingredients	158
	Direction	158
	Nutrition Information	159
78.	Mushroom Cap Chorizo Burger	160
	Ingredients	160
	Direction	160
	Nutrition Information	161
79.	Mushroom Kabobs	162
	Ingredients	162
	Direction	162
	Nutrition Information	163
80.	Mushroom Lasagna with	164
	Ingredients	164
	Direction	164
	Nutrition Information	165
81.	Mushroom Sliders	166
	Ingredients	166
	Direction	166
	Nutrition Information	167
82.	Mushroom Spinach Mac andCheese	168

Ingredients 168
Direction 168
Nutrition Information 169
83. Nayzas Mushroom Fiesta Cups 170
Ingredients 170
Direction 171
Nutrition Information 172
84. Orzo and Chicken Stuffed Peppers 173
Ingredients 173
Direction 174
Nutrition Information 174
85. Pan Fried Fingerling Potatoes with Wild Mushroom Sauce 175
Ingredients 175
Direction 175
Nutrition Information 176
86. Pasta Shells with Portobello Mushrooms and Asparagus in Boursin Sauce 177
Ingredients 177
Direction 177
Nutrition Information 178
87. Pastini Soup 179
Ingredients 179
Direction 179
Nutrition Information 179
88. Penne with Sausage and Portobello Mushrooms 180
Ingredients 180
Direction 180
Nutrition Information 181
89. Penne with Yogurt Tahini Sauce 182
Ingredients 182
Direction 182
Nutrition Information 183
90. Peppered Shrimp Alfredo 184
Ingredients 184

Direction	184
Nutrition Information	185
91. Personal Portobello Pizza	186
Ingredients	186
Direction	186
Nutrition Information	186
92. PestoStuffed GrilledPortobellos	188
Ingredients	188
Direction	188
Nutrition Information	189
93. PizzaStyle PortabelloMushrooms	190
Ingredients	190
Direction	190
Nutrition Information	191
94. Portabella Basil Sub	192
Ingredients	192
Direction	192
Nutrition Information	193
95. Portabello Mushroom andPepper Risotto	194
Ingredients	194
Direction	194
Nutrition Information	195
96. Portobello Artichoke Soup	196
Ingredients	196
Direction	196
Nutrition Information	197
97. Portobello Bellybuttons	198
Ingredients	198
Direction	198
Nutrition Information	198
98. Portobello Bruschetta withThree Cheeses	200
Ingredients	200
Direction	200

Nutrition Information 201
99. Portobello Burgers with GoatCheese 202
Ingredients 202
Direction 202
Nutrition Information 203
100. Portobello Chicken 204
Ingredients 204
Direction 204
Nutrition Information 204
101. Portobello Lemon Chicken 206
Ingredients 206
Direction 206
Nutrition Information 206
102. Portobello MushroomAppetizer 208
Ingredients 208
Direction 208
Nutrition Information 209
103. Portobello MushroomBolognese Sauce 210
Ingredients 210
Direction 210
Nutrition Information 211
104. Portobello Mushroom BurgerWith Bruschetta Topping 212
Ingredients 212
Direction 212
Nutrition Information 213
105. Portobello Mushroom Burgers 214
Ingredients 214
Direction 214
Nutrition Information 214
106. Portobello Mushroom Capsand Veggies 216
Ingredients 216
Direction 216
Nutrition Information 216

107. Portobello Mushroom Chili 218
Ingredients 218
Direction 218
Nutrition Information 218
108. Portobello Mushroom FreshPeppers and Goat Cheese Pizza 220
Ingredients 220
Direction 220
Nutrition Information 221
109. Portobello Mushroom LentilSoup 222
Ingredients 222
Direction 222
Nutrition Information 223
110. Portobello Mushroom Pasta 224
Ingredients 224
Direction 224
Nutrition Information 224
111. Portobello Mushroom Pastawith Basil 226
Ingredients 226
Direction 226
Nutrition Information 227
112. Portobello Mushroom Pizzas 228
Ingredients 228
Direction 228
Nutrition Information 229
113. Portobello Mushroom Ravioliwith Prawns 230
Ingredients 230
Direction 230
Nutrition Information 231
114. Portobello Mushroom Sauce 232
Ingredients 232
Direction 232
Nutrition Information 232
115. Portobello MushroomStroganoff 233

Ingredients 233
Direction 233
Nutrition Information 234
116.   Portobello Penne PastaCasserole 235
Ingredients 235
Direction 235
Nutrition Information 236
117.   Portobello Pesto Egg Omelette 237
Ingredients 237
Direction 237
Nutrition Information 238
118.   Portobello Port Sauce forSteak 239
Ingredients 239
Direction 239
119.   Portobello Pot Pie 240
Ingredients 240
Direction 240
Nutrition Information 241
120.   Portobello Sandwiches 242
Ingredients 242
Direction 242
Nutrition Information 243
121.   Portobello Stacks 244
Ingredients 244
Direction 244
Nutrition Information 244
122.   Portobello Stuffed MushroomBurger 246
Ingredients 246
Direction 246
Nutrition Information 247
123.   Portobello Wild Rice andGizzards 248
Ingredients 248
Direction 248

Nutrition Information 249
124. Pumpkin Lasagna 250
Ingredients 250
Direction 250
Nutrition Information 251
125. Roasted Portabello Mushrooms with Blue Cheese 252
Ingredients 252
Direction 252
Nutrition Information 252
126. Roasted Portobello MushroomFettuccine 254
Ingredients 254
Direction 254
Nutrition Information 255
127. Roasted Portobello Red Pepper and Arugula Salad forOne 257
Ingredients 257
Direction 257
Nutrition Information 258
128. Roasted Vegetable Orzo 259
Ingredients 259
Direction 259
Nutrition Information 260
129. Roasted Vegetables with Walnuts Basil and BalsamicVinaigrette 261
Ingredients 261
Direction 261
Nutrition Information 262
130. Root Veggie Casserole 263
Ingredients 263
Direction 263
Nutrition Information 264
131. Sauceless Garden Lasagna 265
Ingredients 265
Direction 265
Nutrition Information 266

132. Sausage Mushroom and Cranberry Tart 267
Ingredients 267
Direction 267
Nutrition Information 268
133. Sauteed Mushrooms Quick and Simple 269
Ingredients 269
Direction 269
Nutrition Information 269
134. Sauteed Portobellos and Spinach 271
Ingredients 271
Direction 271
Nutrition Information 271
135. Savannahs Best Marinated Portobello Mushrooms 273
Ingredients 273
Direction 273
Nutrition Information 273
136. Savory Portobello Mushroom Burgers 275
Ingredients 275
Direction 275
Nutrition Information 276
137. Savory Swiss Chard with Portobellos 277
Ingredients 277
Direction 277
Nutrition Information 278
138. Scallop Topped Portabello Mushrooms 279
Ingredients 279
Direction 279
Nutrition Information 280
139. Seafood Lasagna II 281
Ingredients 281
Direction 281
Nutrition Information 282
140. Seared Salmon with Indian Inspired Cream Sauce 283

Ingredients 283
Direction 283
Nutrition Information 284
141. Shrimp and PortobelloMushroom Fettuccine 285
Ingredients 285
Direction 285
Nutrition Information 286
142. Slow Cooker Cornish Hens 287
Ingredients 287
Direction 287
Nutrition Information 287
143. South Dakota Wild MushroomDip 289
Ingredients 289
Direction 289
Nutrition Information 290
144. Spaghetti Bolognese 291
Ingredients 291
Direction 291
Nutrition Information 292
145. Spicy Chicken Orecchiette 293
Ingredients 293
Direction 293
Nutrition Information 294
146. Spicy Sweetbreads 295
Ingredients 295
Direction 295
Nutrition Information 296
147. Spinach and MushroomFrittata 297
Ingredients 297
Direction 297
Nutrition Information 297
148. Spinach Stuffed PortobelloMushrooms 299
Ingredients 299

Direction	299
Nutrition Information	300
149. Spinach Stuffed PortobelloMushrooms with Avocado	301
Ingredients	301
Direction	301
Nutrition Information	302
150. Stuffed Portobello Mushrooms	303
Ingredients	303
Direction	303
Nutrition Information	303
151. Summer Vegetarian Chili	305
Ingredients	305
Direction	305
Nutrition Information	306
152. Swedish Turkey Meatballs	307
Ingredients	307
Direction	308
Nutrition Information	308
153. Teresas Hearty ChickenCacciatore	309
Ingredients	309
Direction	310
Nutrition Information	311
154. Tofu and Portobello MushroomParmigiana	312
Ingredients	312
Direction	312
Nutrition Information	313
155. Turkey Mushroom Gravy	314
Ingredients	314
Direction	314
Nutrition Information	315
156. Turkey Portobello Pizza	316
Ingredients	316
Direction	316

Nutrition Information 317
157.   Vegan Portobello Stroganoff 318
Ingredients 318
Direction 318
Nutrition Information 319
158.   Vegan Spaghetti 320
Ingredients 320
Direction 320
Nutrition Information 321
159.   VegetableStuffed PortobelloMushrooms 322
Ingredients 322
Direction 322
Nutrition Information 323
160.   Vegetarian MushroomWalnutMeatloaf 324
Ingredients 324
Direction 324
Nutrition Information 325
161.   Wilted Arugula and PortobelloMushrooms 326
Ingredients 326
Direction 326
Nutrition Information 327
162.   Winter Minestra 328
Ingredients 328
Direction 328
Nutrition Information 329
   Chapter 2: Enoki 330
163.   ABC Ribeye Steak 331
Ingredients 331
Direction 331
Nutrition Information 332
164.   Asian Chicken and Corn Soup 333
Ingredients 333
Direction 333

Nutrition Information 334
165. Bacon Wrapped Delights 335
Ingredients 335
Direction 335
Nutrition Information 336

Chapter 1: Portobello
***

1. # 25Minute Tunisian Vegetable Couscous

"A perfect summer meal. What I love about this recipe is the practicality: it is both quick to make and can wait for you; there's no hurry to serve. It's also a satisfying vegetarian meal that even carnivores love, or if a member of your household prefers meat, a chicken breast poached in water, wine, and paprika and then sliced very thin can be added. I do highly recommend the garnish I devised; it can be made very quickly while the couscous is cooking. Or even if you just zest a navel orange over this dish, the aroma is heavenly and it brings the flavors together. Enjoy!"

Serving: 6 | Prep: 12 m | Cook: 13 m | Ready in: 25 m

Ingredients

- 1 tablespoon olive oil

- 1 red onion, chopped
- 1 zucchini, coarsely chopped
- 1 yellow squash, coarsely chopped
- 1 carrot, coarsely chopped
- 1 red bell pepper, coarsely chopped

- 1 yellow bell pepper, coarsely chopped
- 1/2 cup sliced baby portabella mushrooms
- 4 cups vegetable broth
- 1/2 teaspoon smoked sweet paprika
- 1/4 teaspoon ground cardamom
- 1/4 teaspoon salt
- 1 tablespoon chopped fresh cilantro
- 1 (16 ounce) can chickpeas, drained
- 2 Roma tomatoes, sliced
- 2 cups dry couscous
- 1 teaspoon grated orange zest
- 1 tablespoon grated Parmesan cheese (optional)
- 1/2 teaspoon paprika (optional)
- 1 tablespoon finely chopped toasted almonds (optional)

Direction

- Heat oil in large pot over medium-low heat. Place onion, zucchini, yellow squash, and carrot in pot and cook, stirring occasionally, until onions begin to soften and turn translucent, about 5 minutes. Stir in the red and yellow peppers and mushrooms; cook another 3 minutes. Vegetables should still be firm.
- Pour in the vegetable stock and season with paprika, cardamom, salt, and cilantro. Bring mixture to a boil; reduce heat to low. Stir in chickpeas and tomatoes. Slowly pour in the couscous; stir. Cover pot immediately and remove from the heat. Let stand, covered, for 5 minutes. Fluff couscous with a fork. The couscous should have absorbed about half the cooking liquid.
- Serve at slightly warmer than room temperature. Garnish with orange zest and the grated cheese, paprika, and almonds.

Nutrition Information

- Calories: 387 calories
- Total Fat: 4.9 g
- Cholesterol: < 1 mg
- Sodium: 699 mg
- Total Carbohydrate: 72.1 g
- Protein: 13.6 g

2. Absolutely Fabulous Portobello Mushroom Tortellini

"Gourmet, delicious, and so easy - what could be better? A must for impromptu dinner guests."

Serving: 4 | Prep: 10 m | Cook: 15 m | Ready in: 25 m

Ingredients

- 1 pound cheese tortellini
- 2 large portobello mushrooms
- 1/4 cup white wine
- 1 tablespoon chopped fresh parsley
- 2 cloves garlic, minced
- 8 ounces Alfredo-style pasta sauce
- salt and pepper to taste
- 1/3 cup grated Parmesan cheese

Direction

- Bring a large pot of lightly salted water to a boil. Add pasta and cook for 8 to 10 minutes or until al dente; drain.
- Meanwhile, prepare mushrooms by rinsing and thinly slicing the mushroom caps; discard the stems.
- In a medium skillet over low heat, combine wine, parsley, garlic and mushrooms; stirring frequently, sauté for approximately 5 minutes or until mushrooms are cooked through.
- Remove skillet from heat and slowly add Alfredo sauce, stirring to blend; season with salt and pepper to taste.
- Separate hot pasta into four portions and spoon sauce over pasta. Garnish with cheese and serve immediately.

Nutrition Information

- Calories: 470 calories
- Total Fat: 25.4 g
- Cholesterol: 55 mg
- Sodium: 933 mg
- Total Carbohydrate: 42.2 g
- Protein: 18.3 g

3. All Day Venison Pot Roast

"My step-daughters always refused to eat venison, so we had to come up with creative ways to disguise it. This very tender and savory slow cooker pot roast always had them coming back for more. It wasn't until years later we revealed the truth of the roast's origins! Serve roast, vegetables and gravy over mashed potatoes."

Serving: 6 | Prep: 15 m | Cook: 8 h | Ready in: 8 h 15 m

Ingredients

- 3 onions, chopped
- 5 carrots, cut into 2-inch pieces
- 1 cup chopped portobello mushrooms
- 3 pounds venison rump roast
- 2 garlic cloves, crushed
- 1 tablespoon ground black pepper
- salt to taste (optional)
- 1 (10.75 ounce) can condensed cream of mushroom soup
- 1 (10.5 ounce) can condensed beef broth

- 1/4 cup water
- 1 (1.25 ounce) envelope dry onion gravy mix

Direction

- Arrange the onions, carrots, and mushrooms in the bottom of a slow cooker. Rub the venison rump roast with garlic, black pepper, and salt, then place on top of the vegetables. Mix the cream of mushroom soup, beef broth, water, and onion gravy mix in a bowl until gravy mix is dissolved; pour soup mixture over the roast.
- Cook on High setting until roast is very tender, 8 to 10 hours. Slice roast before serving with gravy and vegetables.

Nutrition Information

- Calories: 343 calories
- Total Fat: 7.9 g
- Cholesterol: 161 mg
- Sodium: 1043 mg
- Total Carbohydrate: 19.6 g
- Protein: 47 g

4. Asparagus and Mushroom Quiche

"This delicious symphony of asparagus, portobello mushrooms, crispy bacon and onion will leave your taste buds hungry for more. Perfect for breakfast, brunch, lunch or dinner."

Serving: 6 | Prep: 25 m | Cook: 35 m | Ready in: 1 h

Ingredients

- 5 slices bacon
- 2 tablespoons olive oil
- 1 small onion, cut into 1/2-inch pieces
- 1 cup portobello mushrooms, stem and ribs removed, cut into 1-inch pieces
- 1 cup chopped fresh asparagus
- 1 (8 inch) unbaked pie shell
- 1 egg white, lightly beaten (optional)
- 1 cup shredded sharp Cheddar cheese
- 1/4 cup crumbled feta cheese
- 2 eggs
- 3/4 cup half-and-half cream
- 1/2 teaspoon salt
- Fresh ground pepper

Direction

- Preheat oven to 400 degrees F (200 degrees C).
- Cook bacon in a large skillet over medium heat until evenly brown and crisp. Drain on paper towels, crumble and set aside.

- Heat oil in a large skillet over medium-high heat. Add onions; cook and stir until translucent. Reduce the heat to medium and add the portobello mushrooms. Continue cooking until the mushrooms are tender. Set aside.
- Bring a saucepan of salted water to a boil over high heat. Cook asparagus in boiling water until just tender, 1 to 2 minutes. Immediately drain and run under cold water to cool.
- Brush the pie shell with the beaten egg white, if using. Place the onion and mushroom mixture, asparagus, and bacon into the bottom of the pie shell. Sprinkle the Cheddar and feta cheeses over the vegetables. In a small bowl, whisk together the eggs, cream, salt, and pepper until smooth. Pour this mixture over the vegetable and cheese filling.
- Bake uncovered for 35 to 40 minutes, or until firm and lightly browned on top. Let cool to room temperature before serving.

Nutrition Information

- Calories: 368 calories
- Total Fat: 28.3 g
- Cholesterol: 115 mg
- Sodium: 788 mg
- Total Carbohydrate: 13.5 g
- Protein: 15.4 g

5. Asparagus Portobello Pasta

"Tasty pasta covered in an asparagus based sauce with sauteed portobello mushrooms and peas."

Serving: 4 | Prep: 10 m | Cook: 20 m | Ready in: 30 m

Ingredients

- 2 (15 ounce) cans asparagus
- 1 (2.25 ounce) can sliced black olives
- 1/2 pound fettuccini pasta
- 1 tablespoon olive oil
- 3 large portobello mushrooms, sliced
- 1 (8 ounce) can peas, drained
- 2 teaspoons Italian seasoning
- 1 (6 ounce) can tomato paste
- 1/2 cup grated Parmesan cheese

Direction

- Fill a large pot with water and the drained liquids of the asparagus and the olives; bring to a boil. Cook pasta for 8 to 10 minutes, or until al dente. Drain.
- Meanwhile, heat oil in a large skillet over medium heat. Sauté mushrooms, peas, and Italian seasoning until mushrooms are tender.
- In a blender or food processor, puree asparagus, black olives, tomato paste and Parmesan. Transfer to a small saucepan, and heat through over medium-low heat. Spoon asparagus sauce over fettuccini, and top with mushrooms and peas.

Nutrition Information

- Calories: 390 calories
- Total Fat: 10.1 g
- Cholesterol: 9 mg
- Sodium: 1248 mg
- Total Carbohydrate: 61.5 g
- Protein: 19.6 g

6. Baked Asparagus with Portobello Mushrooms and Thyme

"Asparagus and portobello mushroom work great together, especially when baked in the oven. You can use any herbs you like, but our family loves thyme."

Serving: 4 | Prep: 10 m | Cook: 15 m | Ready in: 25 m

Ingredients

- 2 pounds fresh asparagus, trimmed
- 2 portobello mushroom caps, cut into strips
- 2 tablespoons olive oil
- 3 sprigs fresh thyme, leaves removed
- salt and freshly ground black pepper

Direction

- Preheat the oven to 450 degrees F (230 degrees C). Lightly grease a baking sheet.
- Combine asparagus and portobello mushrooms in a bowl and drizzle with olive oil. Season with thyme, salt, and pepper. Mix well to combine. Spread in one layer on the prepared baking sheet.
- Bake in the preheated oven until asparagus is tender, about 8 minutes. Turn and bake for an additional 8 to 12 minutes, depending on the thickness of asparagus spears. Season with salt and pepper.

Nutrition Information

- Calories: 109 calories
- Total Fat: 7.1 g
- Cholesterol: 0 mg
- Sodium: 44 mg
- Total Carbohydrate: 9.6 g
- Protein: 5.4 g

7. Baked Mushrooms and Potatoes with Spinach

"This is a tasty, thrifty comfort food which is healthy and can be changed to fit any lifestyle. Add some cheese or bacon bits for a different twist."

Serving: 4 | Prep: 20 m | Cook: 25 m | Ready in: 45 m

Ingredients

- 1 pound new potatoes, halved
- 2 tablespoons olive oil
- 1/2 pound portobello mushrooms
- 6 cloves unpeeled garlic
- 2 tablespoons chopped fresh thyme
- 1 tablespoon olive oil
- kosher salt and ground black pepper to taste
- 1/4 pound cherry tomatoes
- 2 tablespoons toasted pine nuts
- 1/4 pound spinach, thinly sliced

Direction

- Preheat oven to 425 degrees F (220 degrees C).
- Place new potatoes in a shallow roasting pan; drizzle with 2 tablespoons of olive oil. Roast for 15 minutes, turning once.
- Add portobello mushrooms, placing stem sides up, and garlic cloves to pan. Sprinkle with chopped thyme. Drizzle with 1 tablespoon olive oil and season with kosher salt and black pepper. Return to oven; cook 5 minutes.

- Remove pan from oven and add cherry tomatoes. Return to oven; cook until mushrooms are softened, about 5 more minutes.
- Scatter pine nuts over potatoes and mushrooms. Serve with sliced spinach.

Nutrition Information

- Calories: 236 calories
- Total Fat: 12.8 g
- Cholesterol: 0 mg
- Sodium: 136 mg
- Total Carbohydrate: 27.4 g
- Protein: 6.1 g

8. Baked Pasta with Sausage and Baby Portobello Mushroom White Sauce

"This easy to make dish will impress your family or friends with its exotic flavors. This recipe will have your friends and family coming back for more!"

Serving: 12 | Prep: 15 m | Cook: 20 m | Ready in: 35 m

Ingredients

- 1 pound penne pasta
- 3 tablespoons extra-virgin olive oil, divided
- 1 pound bulk Italian sausage
- 1 pound cremini mushrooms, sliced
- 3 cloves garlic, minced
- 1 1/2 cups heavy cream
- 1/4 teaspoon salt, or to taste
- 1/4 teaspoon cracked black pepper
- 1/2 cup grated Parmesan cheese
- 1 (8 ounce) package shredded whole milk mozzarella

Direction

- Preheat the oven's broiler and set the oven rack about 6 inches from the heat source.
- Bring a large pot of lightly-salted water to a boil; cook the penne uncovered, stirring occasionally, until tender yet firm to the bite, about 11 minutes. Drain and return to the pot.
- Meanwhile, heat 1 tablespoon of the olive oil in a large skillet over medium-high heat. Cook and stir the sausage in the hot oil

until crumbly and no longer pink, about 7 minutes: remove from the skillet, leaving the fat in the pan, and set aside. Pour the remaining 2 tablespoons of olive oil into the skillet and add the mushrooms and garlic. Cook and stir until the mushrooms have browned and begun to release their liquid, about 5 minutes more. Return the sausage to the skillet and pour in the heavy cream. Season with salt and pepper and return to a simmer, cooking until the sauce begins to thicken, about 5 minutes more. Pour the sauce over the pasta and stir. Stir in 1/2 cup mozzarella and Parmesan. Pour into a 9x13-inch baking dish and sprinkle with remaining 1/2 cup mozzarella cheese.
- Broil in the preheated oven until the mozzarella cheese is bubbly and golden brown, 5 to 7 minutes.

Nutrition Information

- Calories: 440 calories
- Total Fat: 27.4 g
- Cholesterol: 73 mg
- Sodium: 469 mg
- Total Carbohydrate: 31.6 g
- Protein: 17 g

9. Beef Stew with Ale

"A delicious stew with a good brown lager flavor."

Serving: 12 | Prep: 30 m | Cook: 3 h | Ready in: 3 h 30 m

Ingredients

- 2 pounds beef brisket, trimmed and cut into 2-inch pieces
- salt and black pepper to taste
- 2 tablespoons all-purpose flour
- 5 tablespoons canola oil
- 2 cups diced portobello mushroom caps
- 1 1/2 cups red pearl onions, peeled
- 1 cup diced carrot
- 1 cup diced celery root (celeriac)
- 1 cup diced turnip
- 2 cloves garlic, minced
- 2 (12 fluid ounce) cans or bottles brown lager beer
- 2 cups beef broth
- 1 cup diced potato
- 1 tablespoon malt vinegar
- 4 sprigs fresh thyme, chopped
- 2 sprigs fresh rosemary, chopped

Direction

- Place the brisket cubes into a mixing bowl, and season with salt and pepper. Sprinkle with flour, and toss until evenly coated. Heat the canola oil in a Dutch oven or large pot over high heat. Cook the meat in small batches until browned on all

sides; about 5 minutes per batch. Set the meat aside as the batches are done.
- Once the meat has been browned and set aside, stir in the portobello mushrooms, and cook until browned, about 5 minutes. Remove the mushrooms, and set aside. Stir the pearl onions, carrot, celery root, and turnips into the pot. Cook and stir until the onions begin to turn light brown, about 5 minutes. Add the garlic, and continue cooking until the onions are golden brown, about 3 minutes more. Remove the vegetables and set aside.
- Return the beef to the pot, and pour in the beer. Bring to a boil, and cook until the beer has reduced to 1/3 of its original volume, about 8 minutes. Pour in the beef broth and return to a boil. Reduce heat to medium-low, cover, and simmer until the meat starts to become tender, about 1 hour. Return the browned vegetables to the pot along with the potatoes, recover, and cook 1 hour more.
- Stir in the reserved mushrooms, malt vinegar, thyme, and rosemary. Simmer a few minutes until heated through. Season to taste with salt and pepper before serving.

Nutrition Information

- Calories: 224 calories
- Total Fat: 12.5 g
- Cholesterol: 31 mg
- Sodium: 190 mg
- Total Carbohydrate: 13 g
- Protein: 11.1 g

10. Beef Tenderloins with MushroomGarlic Sauce

"Enjoy these hearty beef tenderloin steaks with Progresso™ Recipe Starters™ creamy portabella mushroom cooking sauce--perfect for dinner."

Serving: 4 | Prep: 10 m | Ready in: 40 m

Ingredients

- 3 tablespoons butter
- 4 (7 ounce) beef tenderloin steaks (1 1/2 inches thick)
- 2 cups sliced baby portabella mushrooms
- 4 cloves garlic, finely chopped
- 2 tablespoons dry white wine or beef broth
- 1 (9 ounce) pouch Progresso™ Recipe Starters™ creamy portabella mushroom cooking sauce

Direction

- In 10-inch skillet, melt 1 tablespoon of the butter over medium-high heat. Sprinkle steaks with 1/2 teaspoon salt and 1/4 teaspoon pepper. Cook steaks 4 to 6 minutes, turning once, until deep brown. Reduce heat to low. Cover; cook 6 to 8 minutes for medium-rare to medium doneness (don't overcook; beef will continue to cook while standing). Remove beef to platter; cover to keep warm.
- Increase heat to medium. Add remaining 2 tablespoons butter to skillet. Add mushrooms. Cook 3 to 4 minutes, stirring once or twice and scraping up any browned bits, until tender. Add wine

and cooking sauce; heat to boiling. Reduce heat; simmer 3 to 5 minutes, stirring occasionally, until sauce is hot.
- Serve mushroom sauce over steaks.

Nutrition Information

- Calories: 394 calories
- Total Fat: 23.6 g
- Cholesterol: 122 mg
- Sodium: 359 mg
- Total Carbohydrate: 6.7 g
- Protein: 35.2 g

11. Beths Portobello Mushroom Burgers

"This is a quick, delicious and healthy way to enjoy an American classic!"

Serving: 2 | Prep: 5 m | Cook: 15 m | Ready in: 20 m

Ingredients

- 2 portobello mushroom caps
- 4 slices turkey bacon
- 3 teaspoons horseradish sauce
- 2 leaves romaine lettuce
- 2 slices tomato
- 2 hamburger buns

Direction

- Preheat oven to 450 degrees F (230 degrees C). Line a cookie sheet with foil, and spray it with cooking spray. With a damp cloth, wipe the mushrooms making sure to get off any excess dirt. Trim the stem so the mushroom will sit even like a hamburger.
- Wrap 2 pieces of turkey bacon around each mushroom, tucking the ends under the stem. Place the mushrooms on the cookie sheet. Bake for 10 to 15 minutes. Remove mushrooms from cookie sheet to paper towel to drain.
- Spread 1 1/2 teaspoons of the horseradish sauce over each of the buns (adjust to your own taste). Place 1 piece of lettuce and 1 slice tomato onto each bun. Place one mushroom burger on each bun.

Nutrition Information

- Calories: 313 calories
- Total Fat: 15.3 g
- Cholesterol: 53 mg
- Sodium: 934 mg
- Total Carbohydrate: 29.9 g
- Protein: 15.5 g

12. Broccoli Rabe with Portobello Mushroom

"I have had complaints (Okay...my wife) about the way I used to cook broccoli rabe in oil because I use a lot of garlic and it was too heavy and oily. Check out this version - Lightly steamed broccoli rabe combined with portobello heads - niiiiiice. This recipe yields wonderful broccoli rabe in oil, combined with delicious portobellos, but since the broccoli is cooked separately it is not so heavy with oil. Really nice. Still use plenty of garlic though!!!!"

Serving: 6 | Prep: 20 m | Cook: 40 m | Ready in: 1 h

Ingredients

- 1/2 cup extra-virgin olive oil
- 3 cloves garlic, minced
- 1/2 cup red onion, chopped
- 3 sprigs fresh thyme, chopped
- 2 portobello mushroom caps, cut into 1/4-inch pieces
- sea salt and freshly ground black pepper to taste
- 2 bunches broccoli rabe, ends trimmed, and cut into 2-inch pieces
- 1/4 cup grated Parmesan cheese, or as needed

Direction

- Heat the olive oil in a large skillet over medium heat. Stir in the garlic and onion, and cook until the onion has softened, and the garlic begins to brown, about 10 minutes. Stir in the thyme and portobello mushrooms, then turn the heat to low. Season to taste with salt and pepper, and cook until the mushrooms have reduced but are not browning, 30 to 35 minutes.

- Place a steamer insert into a saucepan, and fill with water to just below the bottom of the steamer. Cover, and bring the water to a boil over high heat. Add the broccoli rabe, recover, and steam until tender, about 6 minutes. Once the broccoli rabe has cooked, toss it with the mushroom mixture, and sprinkle with Parmesan cheese to serve.

Nutrition Information

- Calories: 222 calories
- Total Fat: 19.7 g
- Cholesterol: 3 mg
- Sodium: 130 mg
- Total Carbohydrate: 7.4 g
- Protein: 5.1 g

13. Broccoli Salad with Margarita Dressing

"A quick salad that is made with raw broccoli, romaine lettuce, cherry tomatoes, and a few other ingredients that marinate in a simple olive oil and lime dressing. Perfect way to use up all those cherry tomatoes in the garden."

Serving: 6 | Prep: 20 m | Ready in: 2 h 20 m

Ingredients

- 1 head broccoli, chopped
- 2 cups torn romaine lettuce
- 1 1/2 cups grape tomatoes
- 1 1/2 cups sliced baby portobello mushrooms
- 1 small red onion, sliced
- 1/4 cup extra-virgin olive oil
- 1/4 cup fresh lime juice
- 2 tablespoons honey
- 1 tablespoon chopped fresh cilantro
- 1 teaspoon ground cumin
- salt and ground black pepper to taste
- 1/4 cup shredded white Cheddar cheese

Direction

- Mix broccoli, romaine lettuce, grape tomatoes, mushrooms, and red onion in a large bowl with a lid.
- Place olive oil, lime juice, honey, cilantro, cumin, salt, and black pepper in a blender; blend until smooth.
- Pour lime dressing over vegetables; toss to combine.

- Cover and refrigerate salad for at least 2 hours before topping with white Cheddar cheese and serving.

Nutrition Information

- Calories: 167 calories
- Total Fat: 11.4 g
- Cholesterol: 5 mg
- Sodium: 54 mg
- Total Carbohydrate: 14.8 g
- Protein: 4 g

14. Cabbage with Portobello Mushrooms

"As the mushrooms cook down, they release a flavorful juice that lends an earthy, rich flavor to strips of soft cabbage."

Serving: 4 | Prep: 10 m | Cook: 15 m | Ready in: 25 m

Ingredients

- 1/2 tablespoon margarine (such as Earth Balance®)
- 1/2 tablespoon olive oil
- 1/2 medium head cabbage - cut into thick, short strips
- 2 portobello mushroom caps, thickly sliced
- 2 pinches kosher salt, or to taste
- ground black pepper to taste
- garlic powder to taste

Direction

- Melt the margarine with the olive oil in a large skillet over medium-high heat. Cook and stir the cabbage in the margarine until soft, about 5 minutes; season with salt, pepper, and garlic powder. Add the mushrooms; continue cooking, stirring frequently, until mushrooms are tender.

Nutrition Information

- Calories: 71 calories
- Total Fat: 3.2 g
- Cholesterol: 0 mg

- Sodium: 240 mg
- Total Carbohydrate: 9.8 g
- Protein: 2.9 g

15. Cajun Chicken Pot Pie

"A delicious creamy chicken pot pie with a little bit of kick. Just add a salad, some bread and you have a wonderful, easy, fast satisfying comfort meal! This can also be made ahead of time."

Serving: 6 | Prep: 15 m | Cook: 1 h | Ready in: 1 h 15 m

Ingredients

- 1 deep dish pastry for double crust
- 2 tablespoons olive oil
- 3 skinless, boneless chicken breast halves, cut into bite size pieces
- salt and ground black pepper to taste
- 1 (8 ounce) package portobello mushrooms, chopped
- 1 (10.75 ounce) can reduced-fat, reduced-sodium condensed cream of chicken soup, undiluted
- 1 (10.75 ounce) can reduced-fat, reduced-sodium cream of mushroom soup, undiluted
- 1/2 cup chicken broth, or more as needed
- 1 (8 ounce) package cream cheese, softened
- 1/2 (14.5 ounce) can chopped tomatoes, drained
- 3 cups frozen mixed vegetables, thawed
- 1/4 teaspoon crushed red pepper flakes (optional)

Direction

- Preheat an oven to 375 degrees F (190 degrees C). Spray a deep dish pie pan with cooking spray. Arrange one pie crust on the bottom of the pan.

- Heat the olive oil in a skillet over medium heat. Stir in the chicken breast and season with salt and pepper. Cook and stir until the chicken is no longer pink in the center, about 7 minutes. Add the portobello mushrooms; cook and stir until the mushrooms are tender. Stir in the cream of chicken and cream of mushroom soups, chicken broth, cream cheese, and tomatoes. Stir in more chicken broth if the mixture becomes too thick. Stir in the mixed vegetables and red pepper flakes.
- Pour chicken mixture into the prepared pan, reserving any leftover filling. Place the top crust on top, crimping the edges of the crusts to seal. Poke 4 to 5 holes in the top crust. Cover loosely with aluminum foil.
- Bake in the preheated oven until golden brown, about 45 minutes. Serve with the leftover chicken mixture.

Nutrition Information

- Calories: 655 calories
- Total Fat: 40.4 g
- Cholesterol: 79 mg
- Sodium: 996 mg
- Total Carbohydrate: 49.8 g
- Protein: 23.5 g

16. Callys Omelet

"The best omelet in the world!"

Serving: 2 | Prep: 10 m | Cook: 25 m | Ready in: 35 m

Ingredients

- 2 tablespoons butter
- 1/2 green bell pepper, chopped
- 1/2 red bell pepper, chopped
- 1/2 Bermuda onion, sliced
- 7 baby portobello mushrooms, sliced
- 1/2 pound beef tip
- 1/2 cup egg substitute

Direction

- Melt butter in a medium saucepan over medium heat. Stir in green bell pepper, red bell pepper, onion and portobello mushrooms. Cook until tender, about 5 minutes.
- Stir beef into the vegetable mixture, and cook until evenly brown, 5 to 10 minutes.
- Stir egg beaters into the mixture, and cook 10 minutes, or until firm.

Nutrition Information

- Calories: 511 calories
- Total Fat: 29.5 g
- Cholesterol: 105 mg

- Sodium: 284 mg
- Total Carbohydrate: 26 g
- Protein: 40.2 g

17. Cannelloni Tre Sapori

"Make your own cannelloni by wrapping ground chicken, portobello mushrooms, and eggplant in sheets of fresh pasta. The cannelloni are covered in a mozzarella-white sauce and baked in the oven until golden. A total winner, your family will love it!"

Serving: 6 | Prep: 1 h | Cook: 1 h | Ready in: 2 h

Ingredients

- 1/4 cup butter
- 1/4 cup all-purpose flour
- 2 cups milk
- 12 ounces shredded mozzarella cheese
- 1/2 cup chopped Italian flat leaf parsley
- 2 egg yolks
- Filling:
- 2 tablespoons olive oil
- 2 leeks, finely chopped
- 2 teaspoons minced garlic
- 1/2 cup white wine
- 1 large eggplant, finely chopped
- 2 portobello mushrooms, chopped
- 1 pound ground chicken
- 2 teaspoons minced fresh rosemary
- 4 teaspoons Italian seasoning
- salt and pepper to taste
- 1 pound fresh pasta sheets, cut into 4 inch squares
- 1 cup freshly grated Parmesan cheese

Direction

- Melt butter in a saucepan over medium heat. Stir in flour, and cook until the flour turns from white to a pale beige color, 3 to 4 minutes. Whisk in the milk; cook and stir until the milk has thickened and the flour no longer tastes grainy, about 7 minutes. Remove from the heat and whisk in mozzarella cheese until melted and smooth, then whisk in parsley and egg yolks; set aside and allow to cool.
- Heat olive oil in a large skillet over medium heat; stir in leeks and garlic and cook until the leek has softened and turned translucent, about 4 minutes. Pour in white wine, and allow to cook until evaporated. Mix the leeks together with the eggplant, mushrooms, and ground chicken in a medium bowl. Season with rosemary, Italian seasoning, salt, and pepper; mix until evenly blended and set aside.
- Bring a large pot of lightly salted water to a boil. Add pasta and cook for 2 to 3 minutes or until al dente; drain and rinse under cold running water to chill, set aside.
- Preheat oven to 350 degrees F (175 degrees C).
- Spread about 1 cup of the white sauce in the bottom of a 9x13 inch glass baking dish. Assemble the cannelloni by placing a small amount of filling onto a pasta square, then rolling it into a firm cylinder. Place the cannelloni into the baking dish as you make them. Pour the remaining white sauce overtop, making sure that none of the pasta is uncovered. Sprinkle with Parmesan cheese.
- Bake in preheated oven until the filling has firmed and the sauce has turned bubbly and golden brown. The cannelloni will be ready when the filling reaches 165 degrees F (75 degrees C).

Nutrition Information

- Calories: 730 calories

- Total Fat: 32.4 g
- Cholesterol: 192 mg
- Sodium: 711 mg
- Total Carbohydrate: 57.7 g
- Protein: 49.5 g

18. Chardonnay Chicken Symphony

"A flavorful combination of chicken, Chardonnay, olives, mushrooms, artichoke, and spices for a delightful meal with your sweetheart. Serve promptly while warm as a main dish or optionally over a bed of couscous."

Serving: 3 | Prep: 15 m | Cook: 15 m | Ready in: 30 m

Ingredients

- 1 tablespoon olive oil
- 1 teaspoon salt-free garlic and herb seasoning blend (such as Mrs. Dash®)
- 1/4 teaspoon garlic powder
- 1 pinch ground black pepper
- 6 boneless, skinless chicken breast tenders
- 1 cup dry Chardonnay
- 1 (7 ounce) can portobello mushrooms, drained
- 1 (6 ounce) jar marinated artichoke hearts, drained
- 1 (2.5 ounce) can black olives, drained
- 1/2 teaspoon capers

Direction

- Heat olive oil in a skillet over medium heat.
- Sprinkle salt-free seasoning, garlic powder, and black pepper over both sides of the chicken. Add chicken to the hot skillet; cook for 2 1/2 minutes per side.
- Stir Chardonnay, mushrooms, artichoke hearts, and olives into the skillet. Cook and stir, turning chicken periodically, until no longer pink in the center and the juices run clear, 7 to 10

minutes. An instant-read thermometer inserted into the center should read at least 165 degrees F (74 degrees C).
- Add capers to the skillet, reduce heat, and simmer 3 minutes more.

Nutrition Information

- Calories: 341 calories
- Total Fat: 13.7 g
- Cholesterol: 67 mg
- Sodium: 768 mg
- Total Carbohydrate: 13.7 g
- Protein: 28.2 g

19. Chicken and Portobello Rollups

"Asparagus, portobello mushrooms and red pepper slices are wrapped in a breast of chicken and smothered to your liking of cream of mushroom soup."

Serving: 4 | Prep: 30 m | Cook: 40 m | Ready in: 1 h 10 m

Ingredients

- 1 tablespoon olive oil
- 1 teaspoon minced garlic
- 1 portobello mushroom cap, cut into 1/2-inch slices
- 1 large red bell pepper, cut into strips
- 8 asparagus spears, trimmed
- 1/2 teaspoon seasoned salt
- 1/2 teaspoon dried oregano
- 4 (6 ounce) skinless, boneless chicken breast halves
- 1 (10.5 ounce) can cream of mushroom soup
- 1 cup milk

Direction

- Heat olive oil in a skillet over medium heat. Stir in garlic, and cook until it begins to turn golden brown, about 1 minute. Add the mushroom, red pepper, and asparagus; season with seasoned salt and oregano, then gently cook until softened. Pour mixture onto a plate, and allow to cool.
- Preheat oven to 375 degrees F (190 degrees C). Spray a small, glass baking dish with cooking spray and set aside.

- Place each chicken breast between two sheets of plastic wrap, and pound to 1/4-inch thick. Evenly divide the portobello, red pepper, and asparagus among the flattened chicken breasts. Roll up and secure with toothpicks. Place into prepared baking dish.
- Bake chicken in preheated oven until no longer pink, about 30 minutes. Meanwhile, stir together cream of mushroom soup and milk in a saucepan over medium-high heat. Bring to a simmer, then reduce heat to low, and keep warm while chicken cooks.
- To serve, remove toothpicks from chicken, slice each in half at an angle, and place onto a serving platter or individual plates. Ladle cream of mushroom soup overtop.

Nutrition Information

- Calories: 342 calories
- Total Fat: 13.3 g
- Cholesterol: 102 mg
- Sodium: 709 mg
- Total Carbohydrate: 13.8 g
- Protein: 40.7 g

20. Chicken Artichoke and Spinach Stuffed Portobellos

"These stuffed mushroom caps turn an appetizer into a meal. Serve with a piece of crusty bread and a side salad, if desired. This recipe was made in a Panasonic CIO."

Serving: 4 | Prep: 20 m | Cook: 23 m | Ready in: 43 m

Ingredients

- 1 1/2 pounds skinless, boneless chicken breasts, chopped
- 1 (15 ounce) jar Alfredo sauce
- 1 (10 ounce) package frozen chopped spinach, thawed and squeezed dry
- 1 (7.5 ounce) jar quartered artichoke hearts, drained and chopped
- 1 teaspoon red pepper flakes
- 1 (6 ounce) package shredded Parmesan cheese, divided
- 4 large portobello mushroom caps, stems and gills removed
- 1 tablespoon olive oil
- salt and ground black pepper to taste

Direction

- Combine chicken, Alfredo sauce, spinach, artichoke hearts, red pepper flakes, and 4 ounces of Parmesan cheese in a large bowl. Stir to combine.
- Lightly rub the outside of each portobello with olive oil using your hands; season with salt and pepper.
- Divide the chicken filling among the mushroom caps and top with remaining Parmesan cheese. Place mushroom caps on

the grill pan of the Panasonic Countertop Induction Oven.
- Press "Auto Cook". Select Poultry with Vegetables setting and press "Start". Turn the dial to select 2 pounds and press "Start" again. Cook until chicken is no longer pink and mushrooms are tender, about 23 minutes.

Nutrition Information

- Calories: 762 calories
- Total Fat: 51.1 g
- Cholesterol: 177 mg
- Sodium: 2180 mg
- Total Carbohydrate: 16 g
- Protein: 61.4 g

21. Chicken Marsala Florentine

"This is a gorgeous chicken dish with sun-dried tomatoes, spinach, and mushrooms. It is so wonderful when served with garlic mashed potatoes. It tastes fantastic!"

Serving: 4 | Prep: 10 m | Cook: 25 m | Ready in: 35 m

Ingredients

- 4 boneless, skinless chicken breast halves
- 1/4 cup all-purpose flour
- salt and pepper to taste
- 1 tablespoon dried oregano
- 2 tablespoons olive oil
- 3/4 cup butter
- 3 cups sliced portobello mushrooms
- 3/4 cup sun-dried tomatoes
- 1/2 cup packed fresh spinach
- 1 cup Marsala wine

Direction

- Place chicken breasts between two pieces of wax paper, and pound to 1/4 inch thick with a meat mallet. Dust chicken with flour, salt, pepper and oregano.
- In a skillet, fry chicken in olive oil over medium heat. Cook until done, turning to cook evenly. Set aside, and keep warm.
- In the same pan, melt the butter over medium heat; add mushrooms, sun-dried tomatoes, and Marsala wine. Cook for approximately 10 minutes, stirring occasionally. Mix in spinach, and cook for about 2 minutes. Serve over chicken.

Nutrition Information

- Calories: 671 calories
- Total Fat: 43.4 g
- Cholesterol: 160 mg
- Sodium: 693 mg
- Total Carbohydrate: 24.6 g
- Protein: 32 g

22. Chicken Marsala with Portobello Mushrooms

"A restaurant-style Chicken Marsala with savory portobello mushrooms."

Serving: 6 | Prep: 20 m | Cook: 40 m | Ready in: 1 h

Ingredients

- 8 tablespoons butter, divided
- 2 tablespoons olive oil, divided
- 4 portobello mushroom caps, sliced
- 1 clove garlic, chopped
- 1 tablespoon all-purpose flour
- 1 (14.5 ounce) can beef broth
- 1/2 cup dry Marsala wine
- 1 tablespoon browning sauce
- kosher salt, or to taste
- 1/4 teaspoon ground black pepper, or to taste
- 6 skinless, boneless chicken breast halves - pounded to 1/2 inch thickness
- 1 pinch kosher salt and pepper to taste
- 3/4 cup all-purpose flour, or as needed

Direction

- Preheat oven to 350 degrees F (175 degrees C).
- Melt 4 tablespoons butter and heat 1 tablespoon olive oil in a skillet over medium heat. Cook and stir the mushroom slices in the skillet until tender. Remove pan from heat and set aside.

- Melt 1 tablespoon butter and heat 1 tablespoon olive oil in a saucepan over medium-high heat. Stir in the garlic and cook until tender, then gradually whisk in 1 tablespoon flour. Cook, stirring constantly, for 1 minute.
- Increase heat to high, and whisk in the beef broth, Marsala, and browning sauce. Season sauce with 1/2 teaspoon salt and 1/4 teaspoon pepper. Bring sauce to a boil, and reduce heat to low. Mix in the cooked mushrooms; you'll use the skillet to cook the chicken. Cover saucepan and remove from heat.
- Season chicken with salt and pepper, and dredge chicken breasts in the flour. Over medium heat, melt remaining 3 tablespoons butter in the skillet used to cook the mushrooms. Cook the chicken 2 minutes per side, until browned. Arrange the chicken in the bottom of a 9x13 inch baking dish, and cover with the sauce and mushroom mixture.
- Cover baking dish, and bake 25 minutes in the preheated oven, or until chicken juices run clear.

Nutrition Information

- Calories: 426 calories
- Total Fat: 23.1 g
- Cholesterol: 108 mg
- Sodium: 622 mg
- Total Carbohydrate: 19.9 g
- Protein: 29.1 g

23. Chicken With Portobello Mushrooms and Artichokes

"I asked the man in my life which of my recipes he loved. He knew instantly, but had to describe it since I usually don't name my recipes! It didn't take long before I figured out 'the one with that great sauce' and the smile he gave me, meant this one."

Serving: 4 | Prep: 5 m | Cook: 30 m | Ready in: 35 m

Ingredients

- 4 skinless, boneless chicken breast halves
- 2 tablespoons olive oil
- 1/4 cup all-purpose flour
- salt and pepper to taste
- 1 small onion, thinly sliced
- 2 portobello mushrooms
- 1/2 cup beef broth
- 2 teaspoons dried tarragon
- 5 canned quartered artichoke hearts
- 1/2 cup brandy
- 1/4 cup lemon juice

Direction

- Lightly pound chicken breasts to even thickness. Dust chicken with flour, and add salt and pepper to your taste.
- In a heavy skillet, heat 1 tablespoon olive oil over medium heat. Place chicken in pan, brown on both sides, and cook through; this will take about 8 to 10 minutes. Remove from pan, and set aside.

- Add remaining 1 tablespoon olive oil, and sauté onions and mushrooms over medium heat for 3 to 5 minutes.
- Add beef broth, lemon juice, tarragon, and artichoke hearts to the pan: heat for 2 to 3 minutes, stirring gently. Stir in brandy, and simmer for an additional 2 to 3 minutes. Return chicken to the pan, and heat through.

Nutrition Information

- Calories: 344 calories
- Total Fat: 8.6 g
- Cholesterol: 68 mg
- Sodium: 290 mg
- Total Carbohydrate: 13.7 g
- Protein: 30.9 g

24. ChineseStyle Baby Bok Choy with Mushroom Sauce

"This is a delicious dish. It is an authentic Chinese recipe that I use for my cooking. Baby bok choy and mushroom are the two main ingredients. "

Serving: 8 | Prep: 20 m | Cook: 15 m | Ready in: 35 m

Ingredients

- 2 tablespoons oyster sauce
- 1 tablespoon soy sauce
- 2 teaspoons brown sugar
- 1 teaspoon potato starch
- 1 tablespoon water
- 2 pinches salt
- 1/4 teaspoon vegetable oil
- 4 heads baby bok choy
- 3 tablespoons olive oil
- 2 tablespoons minced green onion
- 1 tablespoon minced garlic
- 1 (8 ounce) package sliced portobello mushrooms

Direction

- In a bowl, mix together the oyster sauce, soy sauce, and brown sugar until the sugar has dissolved. Mix the potato starch and water in a small bowl, and stir it into the oyster sauce mixture until smooth.
- Fill a pot with water, bring to a boil, and stir in salt and vegetable oil. Place the bok choy into the boiling water, and

cook until tender, shiny, and bright green, 2 to 3 minutes. Drain the bok choy, and arrange attractively on a serving platter.
- Heat the olive oil in a large skillet or wok until the oil shimmers, then toss the green onion and garlic in the hot oil until fragrant, about 20 seconds; stir in the mushrooms. Cook and stir until the mushrooms begin to shrink slightly. Sprinkle the mushrooms lightly with salt. Continue to cook the mushrooms, stirring often, until they are tender, about 5 minutes. Pour in the oyster sauce mixture, then stir until the sauce is thickened and coats the mushrooms, 30 seconds to 1 minute. Pour the thickened mushroom sauce over the bok choy; serve immediately.

Nutrition Information

- Calories: 69 calories
- Total Fat: 5.4 g
- Cholesterol: 0 mg
- Sodium: 175 mg
- Total Carbohydrate: 4.7 g
- Protein: 1.7 g

25. Couscous with Mushrooms and SunDried Tomatoes

"Lively sun-dried tomatoes and hearty portobello mushrooms are tossed with couscous in this satisfying entree."

Serving: 4 | Prep: 30 m | Cook: 15 m | Ready in: 45 m

Ingredients

- 1 cup dehydrated sun-dried tomatoes
- 1 1/2 cups water
- 1/2 (10 ounce) package couscous
- 1 teaspoon olive oil
- 3 cloves garlic, pressed
- 1 bunch green onions, chopped
- 1/3 cup fresh basil leaves
- 1/4 cup fresh cilantro, chopped
- 1/2 lemon, juiced
- salt and pepper to taste
- 4 ounces portobello mushroom caps, sliced

Direction

- Place the sun-dried tomatoes in a bowl with 1 cup water. Soak 30 minutes, until rehydrated. Drain, reserving water, and chop.
- In a medium saucepan, combine the reserved sun-dried tomato water with enough water to yield 1 1/2 cups. Bring to a boil. Stir in the couscous. Cover, remove from heat, and allow to sit 5 minutes, until liquid has been absorbed. Gently fluff with a fork.

- Heat the olive oil in a skillet. Stir in the sun-dried tomatoes, garlic, and green onions. Cook and stir about 5 minutes, until the green onions are tender. Mix in the basil, cilantro, and lemon juice. Season with salt and pepper. Mix in the mushrooms, and continue cooking 3 to 5 minutes. Toss with the cooked couscous to serve.

Nutrition Information

- Calories: 178 calories
- Total Fat: 2 g
- Cholesterol: 0 mg
- Sodium: 300 mg
- Total Carbohydrate: 36.1 g
- Protein: 7.5 g

26. Cream Cheese Alfredo Sauce

"This is my spin on Alfredo sauce. We love cream cheese, mushrooms and garlic. So I decided to try different ways of creating this tasty dish! Serve with fettuccini, and sliced crusty bread for mopping!"

Serving: 6 | Prep: 10 m | Cook: 15 m | Ready in: 25 m

Ingredients

- 2 tablespoons butter
- 2 portobello mushroom caps, thinly sliced
- 1 (8 ounce) package cream cheese
- 1/2 cup butter
- 1 1/2 cups milk
- 6 ounces grated Parmesan cheese, or to taste
- 1 clove garlic, crushed
- 1 tablespoon minced fresh basil leaves
- ground white pepper, to taste

Direction

- Heat 2 tablespoons of butter in a skillet over medium heat. Stir in the mushrooms; cook and stir until softened, about 5 minutes. Set aside.
- Meanwhile, melt the cream cheese and 1/2 cup of butter in a saucepan over medium heat, stirring occasionally. Stir in the milk and Parmesan cheese, mixing until smooth. Add in the garlic, basil, and white pepper. Simmer for 5 minutes, then remove the garlic. Stir in the cooked mushrooms before serving.

Nutrition Information

- Calories: 464 calories
- Total Fat: 41.6 g
- Cholesterol: 122 mg
- Sodium: 708 mg
- Total Carbohydrate: 7.2 g
- Protein: 16.9 g

27. Creamy Beef Tips with Mushrooms

"Super quick prep and your family will love it! My children are dairy-intolerant; I have found that coconut milk is an excellent substitute for milk and cream and gives any dish a wonderful flavor. This recipe is gluten-free and dairy-free. It is also wonderful served over rice."

Serving: 6 | Prep: 25 m | Cook: 1 h 11 m | Ready in: 1 h 36 m

Ingredients

- 1 (14 ounce) can coconut milk
- 1 cup beef broth
- 8 ounces portobello mushrooms, cleaned and sliced
- 1 green bell pepper, cut into strips
- 1 yellow onion, cut into strips
- 1 teaspoon sea salt
- 1 1/2 pounds beef sirloin tips, cubed
- 1 (16 ounce) package linguine pasta

Direction

- Preheat oven to 400 degrees F (200 degrees C).
- Combine coconut milk, beef broth, portobello mushrooms, green bell pepper, onion, and sea salt in a 9x13-inch casserole dish; mix well. Add beef tips; stir until well-coated.
- Bake in the preheated oven until beef is tender and sauce has thickened, about 1 hour.
- Bring a large pot of lightly salted water to a boil. Cook linguine at a boil until tender yet firm to the bite, about 11 minutes; drain. Serve beef tips and sauce over pasta.

Nutrition Information

- Calories: 594 calories
- Total Fat: 26.2 g
- Cholesterol: 60 mg
- Sodium: 483 mg
- Total Carbohydrate: 60.7 g
- Protein: 31.7 g

28. Crock Pot Portobello Chicken

"We love both portabellos and chicken, and after cooking this same meal on the grill I found a way to bring it inside via the crock pot. Two different preparations - same great results. Even after working all day, we serve guests a meal that gives the impression I cooked all day!"

Serving: 4 | Prep: 10 m | Cook: 6 h | Ready in: 6 h 10 m

Ingredients

- 4 frozen bone-in chicken breast halves
- 8 portobello mushroom caps
- 1 (8 ounce) bottle Italian-style salad dressing
- 1 (8 ounce) package angel hair pasta

Direction

- Place the frozen chicken breasts into a slow cooker, and arrange the mushroom caps on top of the chicken so that about half the mushrooms are facing up. Drizzle the dressing over the chicken and mushroom caps.
- Place the lid on the slow cooker, turn it to the Low setting, and cook until the chicken breasts are no longer pink at the bone and the juices run clear, about 6 hours.
- A few minutes before serving, fill a large pot with lightly salted water and bring to a rolling boil over high heat. Stir in the angel hair pasta, and return to a boil. Cook the pasta uncovered, stirring occasionally, until the pasta has cooked through, but is still firm to the bite, 4 to 5 minutes. Drain well in a colander set in the sink.

- Divide the hot, cooked pasta among four plates, top each plate with a chicken breast and two mushroom caps, and drizzle sauce over the top.

Nutrition Information

- Calories: 628 calories
- Total Fat: 23 g
- Cholesterol: 128 mg
- Sodium: 1155 mg
- Total Carbohydrate: 48.2 g
- Protein: 58.6 g

29. Easy Flat Iron Steak in Wine Sauce

"This simple flat iron steak stays tender in a delicious wine sauce, and is a sure jaw dropper."

Serving: 2 | Prep: 15 m | Cook: 20 m | Ready in: 1 h 20 m

Ingredients

- 2 (6 ounce) flat iron steaks
- 2 tablespoons olive oil
- 1/8 teaspoon cayenne pepper, or to taste
- 1 teaspoon ground black pepper
- 1 tablespoon ground paprika
- 1 teaspoon salt
- 1 1/2 teaspoons dry mustard powder
- 1 1/2 teaspoons garlic powder
- 3 tablespoons olive oil
- 1/2 cup dry red wine
- 1 cup sliced portobello mushrooms

Direction

- Allow the steaks to come to room temperature.
- Stir together 2 tablespoons of olive oil, cayenne pepper, black pepper, ground paprika, salt, mustard powder, and garlic powder in a small bowl to make a paste.
- Prick steaks all over with a fork and rub them well with the spice rub paste, working the rub into the meat.

- Heat a large, heavy skillet over high heat and add the remaining 3 tablespoons of olive oil. Heat oil until it just begins to smoke and quickly sear the steaks until the outside has browned but the center is still blood red and just warmed, 2-3 minutes per side. An instant-read thermometer inserted into the center should read 115 degrees F (46 degrees C).
- Remove steaks from skillet with tongs. Pour the dry red wine into the skillet, and bring to a boil while scraping the browned bits of food off of the bottom of the pan with a wooden spoon. Stir in the sliced portobello mushrooms, and cook and stir until mushrooms are cooked and have released their liquid, about 5 minutes.
- Return steaks to the skillet on top of the mushroom-wine sauce. Reduce heat to LOW and cook until sauce reduces and thickens, about 5 minutes. Remove steaks to serving platter and pour mushroom sauce over steaks to serve.

Nutrition Information

- Calories: 711 calories
- Total Fat: 54.7 g
- Cholesterol: 116 mg
- Sodium: 1280 mg
- Total Carbohydrate: 8.6 g
- Protein: 37.8 g

30. Easy Mushroom Risotto with Trader Joes Cream of Mushroom Soup

"Creamy rice with excellent mushroom flavor. Serves 6 to 8 as a side or 4 as a main dish."

Serving: 6 | Prep: 15 m | Cook: 28 m | Ready in: 43 m

Ingredients

- 4 3/4 cups vegetable broth
- 2 cups Arborio rice
- 1 tablespoon olive oil
- 1 small onion, chopped
- 1 tablespoon minced garlic
- 1 (10 ounce) package sliced baby portobello mushrooms
- salt and ground black pepper to taste
- 11 ounces condensed cream of mushroom soup (such as Trader Joe's® Condensed Cream of Portabella Mushroom Soup)

Direction

- Mix broth and rice together in a pot and bring to a boil. Reduce heat to low and simmer, covered, until broth is absorbed, about 20 minutes. Remove from heat.
- Heat olive oil in a skillet over medium heat; add onion and garlic. Cook until nearly soft, about 3 minutes. Add mushrooms. Cook until they reach your desired texture, 5 to 7 minutes.

Remove from heat and season with salt and pepper, reserving excess liquid.
- Transfer the mushroom mixture to the pot with the rice. Add cream of mushroom soup and stir together evenly.

Nutrition Information

- Calories: 375 calories
- Total Fat: 5.8 g
- Cholesterol: 0 mg
- Sodium: 725 mg
- Total Carbohydrate: 71.9 g
- Protein: 8 g

31. Easy Portobello Mushroom Saute

"This quick and easy recipe tastes so good! You can substitute shallots for the onions if you wish. My family loves this recipe."

Serving: 2 | Prep: 10 m | Cook: 5 m | Ready in: 15 m

Ingredients

- 3 tablespoons olive oil, divided
- 1 1/2 tablespoons garlic flavored olive oil
- 1/4 onion, cut into chunks
- 2 portobello mushroom caps, sliced
- salt and black pepper to taste
- freshly grated Parmesan
- freshly grated Asiago cheese

Direction

- Warm 1 1/2 tablespoons olive oil and 1 1/2 tablespoons garlic flavored olive oil in a skillet over medium heat. Stir in onions and mushrooms; reduce heat to low, and cook until the mushrooms are soft and blackened and the onions are black around the edges. (Add additional olive oil as needed.) Turn the heat off, drizzle with 1 1/2 tablespoons olive oil, and season with salt and pepper. Sprinkle generously with Parmesan and Asiago cheeses.

Nutrition Information

- Calories: 349 calories
- Total Fat: 34 g
- Cholesterol: 10 mg
- Sodium: 166 mg
- Total Carbohydrate: 7.2 g
- Protein: 6.6 g

32. Exotic Mushroom and Walnut Pate

"I got this recipe from a winery at a tasting. It is so delicious on French bread with some wine. For a chunkier consistency, you can fold in additional chopped walnuts at the end. I couldn't stop eating it at the tasting and neither could any of the other tasters!"

Serving: 16 | Prep: 30 m | Cook: 10 m | Ready in: 40 m

Ingredients

- 1 cup walnuts
- 1/2 cup minced shallots
- 1/2 cup unsalted butter
- 1/4 pound shiitake mushrooms, chopped
- 1/4 pound crimini mushrooms, chopped
- 1/4 pound portobello mushrooms, chopped
- 1 tablespoon roasted garlic puree
- 1/4 cup chopped fresh Italian parsley
- 1 tablespoon chopped fresh thyme
- 1/2 teaspoon salt
- 1/2 teaspoon white pepper
- 2 tablespoons extra-virgin olive oil

Direction

- Preheat oven to 350 degrees F (175 degrees C). Spread walnuts in a single layer on a cookie sheet. Toast for 10 minutes, or until fragrant and lightly browned.
- In a large sauté pan, cook shallots in butter over medium heat until translucent. Then add chopped mushrooms, garlic,

parsley, thyme, salt, and pepper. Cook, stirring often, until most of the liquid has evaporated.
- Process toasted walnuts and olive oil in a blender or food processor until mixture forms a thick paste. Spoon in the cooked mushroom mixture, and process to desired texture.
- Pack mixture into well-oiled ramekins or bowl. Cover with plastic wrap, and refrigerate for a few hours or overnight.

Nutrition Information

- Calories: 127 calories
- Total Fat: 12.4 g
- Cholesterol: 15 mg
- Sodium: 80 mg
- Total Carbohydrate: 3.2 g
- Protein: 2.1 g

33. Fettuccine Pasta with Portobello Mushrooms

"This delicious mushroom pasta dish is quick, easy, and delicious - simply ideal for a midweek supper or meat-free Monday. Serve with a salad and some garlic bread."

Serving: 3 | Prep: 10 m | Cook: 15 m | Ready in: 25 m

Ingredients

- 1 (12 ounce) box dry fettuccine pasta
- 2 tablespoons olive oil
- 1/2 onion, minced
- 1 clove garlic, minced
- 1 (8 ounce) package portobello mushrooms, thickly sliced
- 1/4 cup butter
- 3 tablespoons vegetable stock
- 1/2 bunch fresh spinach, finely chopped
- 1 sprig fresh rosemary, chopped, or to taste
- salt and freshly ground black pepper to taste
- 3 tablespoons grated Parmesan cheese

Direction

- Fill a large pot with lightly salted water and bring to a rolling boil. Cook fettuccine at a boil until tender yet firm to the bite, about 8 minutes. Drain.
- Meanwhile, heat olive oil in a skillet over medium heat and cook onion and garlic until soft, about 4 minutes. Add mushrooms and butter; cook and stir until softened, about 3 minutes. Pour in vegetable stock and cook on high heat until

stock has reduced, about 2 minutes. Add spinach and rosemary. Season with salt and pepper. Stir to combine. Add cooked linguine and toss everything to mix well. Cook for an additional 2 to 3 minutes.
- Sprinkle pasta with Parmesan cheese and mix thoroughly. Remove from heat and spoon into warmed bowls.

Nutrition Information

- Calories: 686 calories
- Total Fat: 28.8 g
- Cholesterol: 45 mg
- Sodium: 309 mg
- Total Carbohydrate: 90.8 g
- Protein: 21 g

34. Flat Iron Steak and Spinach Salad

"Spinach is topped with peppers, mushrooms and steak in this recipe."

Serving: 6 | Prep: 25 m | Cook: 25 m | Ready in: 50 m

Ingredients

- 1 (2 pound) flat iron steak
- salt and ground black pepper to taste
- 2 tablespoons olive oil
- 1 large red onion, thinly sliced
- 1/2 cup Italian salad dressing
- 3 large red bell peppers, cut into 1/2 inch strips
- 2 portobello mushrooms, sliced
- 1/2 cup red wine
- 4 cups baby spinach leaves
- 1/2 cup crumbled blue cheese

Direction

- Preheat an outdoor grill for medium-high heat; lightly oil the grate.
- Season the flat iron steak on both sides with salt and pepper. Cook to desired degree of doneness on preheated grill, about 5 minutes per side for medium-rare. Let rest in a warm area while proceeding with the recipe.
- Heat olive oil in a large skillet over medium-high heat. Stir in the onion, and cook until it begins to soften, about 4 minutes. Pour in the Italian salad dressing, and bring to a boil, then stir

in the red peppers and mushrooms. Reduce heat to medium, and cook until the peppers are tender, about 5 minutes.
- Remove the vegetables from the skillet with a slotted spoon, and set aside. Increase the heat to medium-high, and add the red wine. Simmer the salad dressing and wine until it has reduced to a syrupy sauce, about 5 minutes.
- Meanwhile, divide the spinach leaves onto serving plates. Thinly slice the flat iron steak across the grain. Spoon the warm, cooked vegetable mixture over the spinach leaves, then place the sliced steak on top. Spoon on the reduced red wine sauce, and finally, sprinkle with blue cheese.

Nutrition Information

- Calories: 486 calories
- Total Fat: 31.1 g
- Cholesterol: 112 mg
- Sodium: 601 mg
- Total Carbohydrate: 12.7 g
- Protein: 36.2 g

35. Four Cheese Mashed Potato Stuffed Portobello Mushrooms

"Four Cheese Mashed Potato Stuffed Portobello Mushrooms make a fast and filling vegetarian main course hot off the grill or turn this recipe into an appetizer by using cremini mushrooms."

Serving: 4 | Prep: 15 m | Cook: 5 m | Ready in: 20 m

Ingredients

- 1 (4 ounce) package Idahoan® Four Cheese Flavored Mashed Potatoes
- 2 large portobello mushrooms, or more depending on size
- Oil
- Salt and pepper
- 1/2 cup Cheddar cheese, shredded
- 2 tablespoons bell pepper, diced and lightly sautéed
- 2 tablespoons scallions, chopped

Direction

- Preheat oven to 350 degrees F or grill to 400 degrees F.
- Clean the mushrooms and rub with oil.
- Sprinkle with salt and pepper and place on a foil lined baking tray.
- Bake for 5 minutes until tender. Or if grilling, turn mushrooms once or twice while cooking on the grill until tender.
- While mushrooms are cooking, prepare Idahoan Four Cheese Mashed Potatoes according to package instructions.
- Fold in the cheddar cheese and the peppers.

- When mushrooms are cooked, sprinkle with a bit more salt and pepper and stuff with the mashed potatoes.
- Top with the scallions and serve hot.

Nutrition Information

- Calories: 88 calories
- Total Fat: 5.5 g
- Cholesterol: 15 mg
- Sodium: 236 mg
- Total Carbohydrate: 5.6 g
- Protein: 4.1 g

36. French Onion Mushroom Green Beans

"French-cut green beans, sliced sweet onions, mushrooms, and thyme are topped with shredded cheese for a quick, delicious side dish."

Serving: 6 | Prep: 5 m | Cook: 15 m | Ready in: 20 m

Ingredients

- 4 tablespoons Crisco® Pure Vegetable Oil, divided
- 1 large sweet yellow onion, thinly sliced
- 2 tablespoons balsamic vinegar
- 1 (16 ounce) package frozen French cut green beans
- 1 (8 ounce) package sliced baby bella mushrooms
- 1/2 teaspoon dried thyme leaves
- 1/2 teaspoon salt
- 1/2 cup shredded Swiss or Gruyere cheese

Direction

- Heat 2 tablespoons oil in large skillet over medium-low heat. Add onion and vinegar. Cook 15 to 20 minutes or until tender and golden brown. Remove from skillet.
- Heat remaining 2 tablespoons oil in same skillet over medium-high heat. Add green beans, mushrooms and thyme. Cook 4 to 5 minutes, stirring occasionally. Stir in onions and salt. Cook 1 to 2 minutes to until desired doneness. Top with cheese.

Nutrition Information

- Calories: 160 calories
- Total Fat: 12.1 g
- Cholesterol: 8 mg
- Sodium: 219 mg
- Total Carbohydrate: 10.8 g
- Protein: 4.9 g

37. FrenchStyle Stuffed Portobellos with Green Beans

"This is a great 1-skillet meal that oozes with French flavors."

Serving: 3 | Prep: 15 m | Cook: 29 m | Ready in: 44 m

Ingredients

- 2 tablespoons butter, divided
- 1 tablespoon vegetable oil
- 1 small shallot, minced
- 2 cloves garlic, minced
- 3 portobello mushroom caps
- 1/2 pound haricots verts (French green beans), trimmed
- 1/4 cup Sauvignon blanc
- 3 slices Paris ham, or more to taste
- 1/2 cup shredded Gruyère cheese

Direction

- Preheat oven to 375 degrees F (190 degrees C).
- Heat 1 tablespoon butter and oil in an oven-proof skillet over medium heat until butter is melted. Add shallot and garlic; cook and stir until shallot is wilted, about 5 minutes.
- Place mushrooms, gill side up, into the skillet. Cook, flipping once, until liquid is absorbed, 2 to 3 minutes per side. Return mushrooms to gill side up.
- Arrange green beans around the mushrooms. Pour in wine; simmer until absorbed, 5 to 10 minutes. Reduce heat to low;

cover. Cook until mushrooms release their juices and green beans are tender, about 10 minutes.
- Top mushrooms with ham slices; sprinkle evenly with Gruyère cheese. Add remaining 1 tablespoon butter to the green beans.
- Bake in the preheated oven until cheese is melted and bubbly, about 5 minutes.

Nutrition Information

- Calories: 260 calories
- Total Fat: 19.2 g
- Cholesterol: 50 mg
- Sodium: 603 mg
- Total Carbohydrate: 7.1 g
- Protein: 12.2 g

38. Giant Stuffed Mushrooms

"These stuffed mushrooms are too big to serve as hors d'oeuvres.....just one of these enormous mushrooms can be dinner for a hungry person."

Serving: 4

Ingredients

- 4 large portobello mushrooms
- 2 tablespoons olive oil, divided
- salt to taste
- ground black pepper to taste
- 1 clove garlic, minced
- 1 cup chopped fresh cilantro
- 1 large carrot, finely chopped
- 1 stalk celery, finely chopped
- 2/3 cup kasha (toasted buckwheat groats)
- 1 1/4 cups water
- 3 tablespoons chopped fresh parsley

Direction

- Preheat the oven to 400 degrees F (200 degrees C). Remove the mushroom stems from the caps, and set the stems aside. Place the caps gill-side up on a baking sheet. Drizzle them with 1 tablespoon of the olive oil, and season with salt and pepper. Roast in the preheated oven for 25 minutes.
- Meanwhile, prepare the pilaf stuffing. Chop mushroom stems. Heat the remaining olive oil in a skillet over medium heat. Cook chopped mushroom stems and garlic in oil until soft. Stir in the cilantro, carrot, celery and kasha; cook 2 minutes more. Pour in

water. Bring the mixture to a boil, reduce heat to low, and place a lid on the pan. Simmer 20 minutes, or until the kasha is tender. Remove from the heat, and stir in parsley. Season to taste with salt and pepper.
- Stuff the warm mushroom caps with the pilaf, and serve.

Nutrition Information

- Calories: 198 calories
- Total Fat: 7.9 g
- Cholesterol: 0 mg
- Sodium: 328 mg
- Total Carbohydrate: 29.2 g
- Protein: 6.6 g

39. Gourmet Cream Of Wild Mushroom Soup

"This mushroom soup has earthy and creamy flavor. Using a variety of wild mushrooms creates interesting flavors and textures. Serving this soup on special occasions will make the evening unforgettable."

Serving: 4 | Prep: 25 m | Cook: 28 m | Ready in: 53 m

Ingredients

- 3 tablespoons extra-virgin olive oil
- 1 pound assorted wild mushrooms, thinly sliced
- 1 large yellow onion, finely chopped
- 2 portobello mushrooms, thinly sliced
- 1 tablespoon chopped fresh thyme
- 1 teaspoon chopped fresh rosemary
- 1/2 teaspoon sea salt
- 1/4 cup dry white wine
- 3 cups gluten-free chicken broth
- 1 cup heavy whipping cream
- 1/2 cup chopped fresh parsley, divided
- 1 tablespoon gluten-free all-purpose flour
- sea salt and ground white pepper to taste

Direction

- Heat olive oil in a large saucepan over low heat. Add wild mushrooms, yellow onion, portobello mushrooms, thyme, rosemary, and sea salt; cover and cook until mushrooms soften, about 3 minutes.

- Uncover saucepan and pour in white wine; cook and stir until most of the wine evaporates, about 5 minutes. Pour in chicken broth; simmer soup until flavors combine, about 15 minutes.
- Whisk heavy cream, 1/4 cup parsley, and flour together in a small bowl. Pour into the soup; cook, stirring occasionally, until heated through, about 5 minutes. Season soup with salt and pepper; top with remaining 1/4 cup parsley.

Nutrition Information

- Calories: 375 calories
- Total Fat: 33.1 g
- Cholesterol: 85 mg
- Sodium: 1056 mg
- Total Carbohydrate: 13 g
- Protein: 6.7 g

40. Gourmet Gouda Turkey Burgers

"Very flavorful and impressive turkey burger with melted Gouda cheese!"

Serving: 4 | Prep: 20 m | Cook: 10 m | Ready in: 30 m

Ingredients

- 1 egg
- 1/4 cup minced onion
- 1 pound ground turkey
- 1/2 cup fine Italian bread crumbs
- 2 teaspoons liquid smoke flavoring
- 2 tablespoons Worcestershire sauce
- 1/2 teaspoon salt
- 1/2 teaspoon ground black pepper
- 1/4 cup panko bread crumbs
- 1 large portobello mushroom cap, cut into thick slices
- 1 tablespoon olive oil for brushing
- 4 ounces Canadian-style bacon
- 4 ounces sliced Gouda cheese
- 4 hamburger buns, split and toasted
- 1/4 cup spicy brown mustard, or to taste
- 1/2 cup mayonnaise, or to taste

Direction

- Preheat an outdoor grill for medium heat and lightly oil the grate.

- Beat the egg and onion together in a mixing bowl. Add the turkey, Italian bread crumbs, liquid smoke, Worcestershire sauce, salt, and pepper. Mix until evenly combined and form into 4 patties. Press each patty into the panko crumbs and set aside.
- Cook the turkey burgers on the preheated grill until no longer pink in the center and the juices run clear, about 4 minutes per side. An instant-read thermometer inserted into the center should read at least 165 degrees F (74 degrees C). While the burgers are cooking, brush the mushrooms with olive oil and cook on the grill along with the Canadian bacon. Just before the turkey burgers are done, top with the grilled Canadian bacon slices and the Gouda cheese. Cook until the cheese melts.
- Spread the hamburger buns with mustard and mayonnaise. Place a turkey burger onto each bottom bun and top with the portobello mushroom slices. Sandwich with the remaining bun halves and serve.

Nutrition Information

- Calories: 795 calories
- Total Fat: 51 g
- Cholesterol: 187 mg
- Sodium: 1806 mg
- Total Carbohydrate: 41.6 g
- Protein: 44.3 g

41. Great Grilled Smoky Vegetables with Avocado and Goat Cheese Crumbles

"Smoky tender grilled vegetables just bursting with flavor, made pretty with the addition of creamy white goat cheese and luscious avocado! Add any other veggies you like. Asparagus and zucchini are good additions."

Serving: 6 | Prep: 25 m | Cook: 5 m | Ready in: 1 h

Ingredients

- 6 portobello mushroom caps
- 4 red bell peppers, cored and quartered
- 1 red onion, thickly sliced
- 1/2 cup olive oil
- 2 limes, juiced
- 2 tablespoons grill seasoning
- 2 cloves garlic, minced
- 1 pinch cayenne pepper, or to taste
- 2 tablespoons balsamic vinegar
- 1 avocado - peeled, pitted, and cubed
- 1/2 cup crumbled goat cheese
- salt to taste
- freshly ground black pepper to taste
- 2 tablespoons finely chopped fresh basil

Direction

- Place mushrooms, red bell peppers, and red onion in a 9x13-inch baking dish. Whisk olive oil, lime juice, grill seasoning,

garlic, and cayenne pepper in a small bowl; pour over vegetables. Toss to coat and allow vegetables to marinate for at least 30 minutes.
- Preheat grill for medium heat and lightly oil the grate.
- Remove vegetables from the marinade, and shake off excess. Reserve remaining marinade.
- Grill vegetables on preheated grill until tender, about 5 minutes. Transfer grilled vegetables to a large platter. Whisk remaining marinade with balsamic vinegar; pour over vegetables. Top with avocado and goat cheese, then season with salt and pepper. Sprinkle with basil to serve.

Nutrition Information

- Calories: 331 calories
- Total Fat: 27 g
- Cholesterol: 9 mg
- Sodium: 563 mg
- Total Carbohydrate: 18.7 g
- Protein: 7.4 g

42. Green Bean and Portobello Mushroom Casserole

"We got burned out on the traditional recipe. A serious update of the old green bean casserole resulted. It's spicier, not runny, and has an unusual mix of textures. My family loves it! I think yours will too. Can't wait to know what you think."

Serving: 10 | Prep: 15 m | Cook: 35 m | Ready in: 50 m

Ingredients

- 4 slices bacon
- 1/4 cup olive oil
- 1 pound baby portobello mushrooms, sliced
- 1/2 medium onion, chopped
- 3 cloves garlic, finely chopped
- 1/2 cup slivered almonds
- 1 (10.75 ounce) can condensed cream of mushroom soup with roasted garlic
- 3/4 teaspoon seasoned salt with no MSG
- 1/3 teaspoon white pepper
- 2 (15.5 ounce) cans French cut green beans, drained
- 1 cup shredded Cheddar cheese

Direction

- Preheat the oven to 375 degrees F (190 degrees C).
- Place bacon in a large skillet over medium-high heat, and fry until crisp. Remove from the skillet to drain on paper towels. Pour olive oil into the skillet, and reduce heat to medium. When oil is hot, add mushrooms and onion; cook, stirring frequently

until the onions start to become translucent. Add garlic, and fry for a couple of minutes, just until fragrant. Stir in the mushroom soup and almonds, and bring to a boil. Season with seasoned salt and white pepper, and crumble in the bacon. Gently stir in the green beans, then transfer the mixture to a casserole dish.
- Bake uncovered for 30 minutes in the preheated oven. Remove from the oven, and sprinkle Cheddar cheese over the top. Return to the oven for 5 minutes, or until cheese is melted. Let stand 5 minutes before serving.

Nutrition Information

- Calories: 244 calories
- Total Fat: 19.3 g
- Cholesterol: 23 mg
- Sodium: 656 mg
- Total Carbohydrate: 10.3 g
- Protein: 8.5 g

43. Grilled Chicken and Portobello Lasagna Rollups

"A different take on lasagna, these rollups have a filling of grilled chicken breast, sauteed portobello mushrooms, spinach and cheese. They are wonderful with a side salad and hot garlic bread."

Serving: 9 | Prep: 30 m | Cook: 1 h | Ready in: 1 h 30 m

Ingredients

- 18 lasagna noodles, cooked and drained
- 2 cups marinara sauce
- 1 teaspoon vegetable oil
- 2 portobello mushrooms, diced
- 1 cup frozen chopped spinach
- 2 cups diced cooked chicken
- 1 (15 ounce) container ricotta cheese
- 1/2 cup grated Parmesan cheese
- 1 teaspoon dried oregano
- salt and ground black pepper to taste
- 2 cups Alfredo sauce
- 1 cup shredded mozzarella cheese
- 1/4 cup pine nuts

Direction

- Fill a large pot with lightly salted water and bring to a rolling boil over high heat. Stir in the lasagna noodles, and return to a boil. Cook the pasta uncovered, stirring occasionally, until the noodles are cooked, but still firm to the bite, about 8 minutes; drain and rinse.

- Preheat oven to 375 degrees F (190 degrees C). Spread the marinara sauce in the bottom of a 9x13 glass baking dish; set aside.
- Heat oil in a skillet over medium heat; cook and stir mushrooms until they soften, about 5 minutes. Stir in spinach, and cook until hot; remove from heat.
- Stir together the chicken, ricotta cheese, Parmesan cheese, oregano, and the cooked spinach mixture in a large bowl. Season to taste with salt and black pepper. Spread about 1/4 cup of the mixture on each lasagna noodle. Roll the noodle up, and place seam-side down into the prepared baking dish. Repeat for each noodle. Spoon Alfredo sauce over the rollups.
- Bake, covered, in the preheated oven for 40 minutes. Uncover; sprinkle with mozzarella cheese and pine nuts. Return to the oven and bake until the cheese is melted and bubbly and the pine nuts are toasted, about 10 minutes. Serve hot.

Nutrition Information

- Calories: 603 calories
- Total Fat: 32.1 g
- Cholesterol: 74 mg
- Sodium: 1004 mg
- Total Carbohydrate: 50.8 g
- Protein: 30 g

44. Grilled Mushroom and Goat Cheese Rotini with Honey Garlic Chicken Kabobs

"A warm grilled portobello and rotini pasta side dish pairs with honey garlic kabobs in this fusion dish."

Serving: 4 | Prep: 10 m | Cook: 20 m | Ready in: 30 m

Ingredients

- Honey Garlic Chicken Kabobs
- 1 pound boneless skinless chicken breasts, cut into 1-inch cubes
- 1/2 cup VH® Honey Garlic Sauce
- PAM® for Grilling
- 1 large red pepper, cut into 16 chunks
- 1 large green pepper, cut into 16 chunks
- 1 red onion, cut into 16 chunks
- Grilled Mushroom and Goat Cheese Rotini
- 4 medium portobello mushroom caps, gills removed
- 1/4 teaspoon salt
- 1/4 teaspoon ground black pepper
- PAM® Olive Oil or PAM® Original
- 1/2 (12 ounce) package Catelli Bistro® Rotini
- 1 (540 mL) can Aylmer® Accents® Italian Seasonings Chunky Stewed Tomatoes
- 1/2 cup crumbled goat cheese
- 2 tablespoons chopped fresh parsley

Direction

- Honey Garlic Chicken Kabobs: Spray grate of outdoor grill with PAM(R) Grilling for Grill Spray. Preheat grill to medium-high heat.
- Evenly thread chicken, red pepper, green pepper and onion onto 8 skewers. Brush each skewer with VH(R) Honey Garlic Sauce.
- Grill kabobs, turning occasionally, for 15 to 18 minutes or until chicken is cooked through.
- Grilled Mushroom and Goat Cheese Rotini: Preheat grill to medium-high heat. Season mushrooms with salt and pepper; spray with PAM(R) Olive oil or PAM(R) Original. Grill mushrooms for 3 to 5 minutes per side or until grill-marked and tender. Let cool slightly and slice.
- Cook Catelli Bistro(R) Rotini according to package directions; drain, reserving 1/4 cup (60 mL) cooking water.
- Meanwhile, in large, deep skillet, heat Aylmer(R) Accents(R) Italian Seasonings Chunky Stewed Tomatoes over medium heat until simmering. Simmer for 10 minutes. Toss with reserved cooking water, rotini and sliced mushrooms. Top with goat cheese and parsley before serving.

Nutrition Information

- Calories: 532 calories
- Total Fat: 9.1 g
- Cholesterol: 78 mg
- Sodium: 891 mg
- Total Carbohydrate: 77.6 g
- Protein: 37.6 g

45. Grilled Mushroom Sandwich With Citrus Mayo

"I created this recipe to taste like a mushroom sandwich we served at the Good Earth Restaurant in Santa Clara, California (which is no longer in business). It tastes great with marinated portobello mushrooms, roasted red bell peppers, smoked gouda cheese, and spring mix!"

Serving: 4 | Prep: 10 m | Cook: 15 m | Ready in: 55 m

Ingredients

- 2 tablespoons olive oil
- 1/4 cup balsamic vinegar
- 1 clove garlic, minced
- 4 portobello mushroom caps
- 1/3 cup mayonnaise
- 2 tablespoons orange juice
- 1 (12 ounce) jar roasted red bell peppers
- 4 rolls sourdough bread
- 4 slices smoked Gouda cheese
- 1 (10 ounce) bag mixed salad greens

Direction

- Whisk together olive oil, balsamic vinegar, and garlic until well blended. Pour over mushroom caps in a resealable bag to coat, then seal and allow to marinate for 30 minutes. Stir together mayonnaise and orange juice, and set aside.
- Preheat an outdoor grill for medium heat.
- Remove mushroom caps from the marinade and shake off excess. Place each mushroom cap upside down on a square

piece of foil. Place roasted peppers on top, and seal. Cook on preheated grill until tender, about 15 minutes, turning occasionally. When the mushrooms are nearly done, cut open the sourdough rolls and grill until golden brown on the cut sides.
- To assemble the sandwiches, spread the cut sides of the rolls with orange mayonnaise, and layer with mushroom, roasted pepper, Gouda cheese, and the mixed greens.

Nutrition Information

- Calories: 519 calories
- Total Fat: 30.3 g
- Cholesterol: 39 mg
- Sodium: 848 mg
- Total Carbohydrate: 49.2 g
- Protein: 17 g

46. Grilled Portobello and Mozzarella

"Absolutely simple and delicious as an appetizer or main course! Portobello mushrooms with red sauce, roasted red peppers, and mozzarella cheese make this dish just to die for! Yummm!"

Serving: 4 | Prep: 15 m | Cook: 25 m | Ready in: 55 m

Ingredients

- 4 portobello mushroom caps
- 1/2 (8 ounce) bottle Italian salad dressing
- 1 (14 ounce) jar marinara sauce
- 1 (7 ounce) jar roasted red bell peppers, drained and sliced
- 8 slices mozzarella cheese
- 1/2 teaspoon dried oregano
- 1/2 teaspoon dried basil

Direction

- Place the mushrooms in a large resealable plastic bag with the salad dressing. Seal, and marinate for at least 15 minutes.
- Preheat grill for medium-high heat. Heat the marinara sauce in a saucepan over medium heat, and keep warm.
- Oil the grill grate. Place the mushrooms on the grill, and cook for 7 to 10 minutes on each side, until lightly toasted.
- Preheat the oven broiler. Spread the bottom of a shallow baking dish or oven-proof plate with just enough marinara sauce to cover the bottom. Place mushrooms in the dish bottom side up, and top with the peppers and remaining

marinara sauce. Place 2 slices of cheese on each mushroom, and sprinkle with oregano and basil.
- Broil for 3 to 5 minutes, or until the cheese is melted. Serve hot.

Nutrition Information

- Calories: 347 calories
- Total Fat: 19.8 g
- Cholesterol: 38 mg
- Sodium: 1883 mg
- Total Carbohydrate: 25.7 g
- Protein: 18.7 g

47. Grilled Portobello Mushrooms

"A good dish that goes with almost anything year round. You can double this recipe and serve as a main dish with rice. Enjoy!"

Serving: 4 | Prep: 15 m | Cook: 20 m | Ready in: 35 m

Ingredients

- 1/2 cup finely chopped red bell pepper
- 1 clove garlic, minced
- 1/4 cup olive oil
- 1/4 teaspoon onion powder
- 1 teaspoon salt
- 1/2 teaspoon ground black pepper
- 4 portobello mushroom caps

Direction

- Preheat grill for medium heat.
- In a large bowl, mix the red bell pepper, garlic, oil, onion powder, salt, and ground black pepper. Spread mixture over gill side of the mushroom caps.
- Lightly oil the grill grate. Place mushrooms over indirect heat, cover, and cook for 15 to 20 minutes.

Nutrition Information

- Calories: 156 calories
- Total Fat: 13.8 g
- Cholesterol: 0 mg
- Sodium: 589 mg

- Total Carbohydrate: 7.3 g
- Protein: 3.1 g

48. Grilled Portobello Mushrooms with Blue Cheese

"Excellent idea for the grill! Anyone who loves mushrooms or blue cheese will love this recipe. When it is done, its like a mini gourmet pizza. This recipe goes well with grilled steak and grilled asparagus."

Serving: 4 | Prep: 5 m | Cook: 20 m | Ready in: 25 m

Ingredients

- 4 portobello mushrooms, stems removed
- 4 ounces crumbled blue cheese

Direction

- Preheat an outdoor grill for medium-high heat and lightly oil the grate.
- Place mushrooms, gill-side up, on a work surface; fill each with 1 ounce blue cheese.
- Cook mushrooms, blue cheese-side up, on the preheated grill, rotating every 5 minutes, until mushrooms are tender and cheese is melted, about 20 minutes.

Nutrition Information

- Calories: 129 calories
- Total Fat: 8.4 g
- Cholesterol: 21 mg
- Sodium: 402 mg
- Total Carbohydrate: 6.3 g

- Protein: 8.9 g

49. Grilled Portobello Mushrooms with Mashed Cannellini Beans and Harissa Sauce

"This appetizer is loaded with so many flavors and it's vegetarian and healthy. Give it a shot if you want to impress! It may sound like a ton of work, but it really is simple. If you like bold flavors, you will love it!"

Serving: 4 | Prep: 25 m | Cook: 13 m | Ready in: 38 m

Ingredients

- Harissa Sauce:
- 1 roasted red pepper, peeled and minced
- 2 tablespoons chopped shallot
- 1 teaspoon minced garlic
- 1 teaspoon olive oil
- 1 teaspoon chopped fresh mint
- 1 teaspoon lime juice
- 3/4 teaspoon Dijon mustard
- 1/2 teaspoon minced fresh cilantro
- 1/2 teaspoon salt
- 1/4 teaspoon red pepper flakes
- 1 pinch ground coriander
- 1 pinch ground black pepper
- 1 pinch cayenne pepper
- Mashed Beans:
- 2 cups canned cannellini beans
- 2 cups water, or as needed
- 2 teaspoons truffle oil
- 1/2 teaspoon salt

- 1/4 teaspoon ground black pepper
- Portobello Mushrooms:
- 4 large portobello mushroom caps
- 4 teaspoons olive oil
- 1/2 cup vegetable broth
- 1/4 teaspoon salt
- 1/4 teaspoon ground black pepper

Direction

- Mix roasted red pepper, shallot, garlic, 1 teaspoon olive oil, mint, lime juice, Dijon mustard, cilantro, 1/2 teaspoon salt, red pepper flakes, coriander, 1 pinch black pepper, and cayenne pepper together in a bowl to make harissa sauce.
- Combine cannellini beans and water in a small saucepan over medium-low heat; heat until warmed through, about 5 minutes. Drain.
- Combine drained beans, 2 teaspoons truffle oil, 1/2 teaspoon salt, and 1/4 teaspoon pepper in a food processor; puree until smooth.
- Preheat grill for medium heat and lightly oil the grate. Brush mushroom caps on both sides with 4 teaspoons olive oil; season with 1/4 teaspoon salt and 1/4 teaspoon pepper. Grill mushrooms, gill-side up, basting frequently with vegetable broth, about 4 minutes per side.
- Top each mushroom cap with 1/2 cup bean puree and 2 tablespoons of harissa sauce.

Nutrition Information

- Calories: 312 calories
- Total Fat: 10 g

- Cholesterol: 0 mg
- Sodium: 1192 mg
- Total Carbohydrate: 44.8 g
- Protein: 17.1 g

50. Grilled Portobello Sandwich with Roasted Red Pepper and Mozzarella

"I had this once in a restaurant, and have spent a while trying to recreate it. Please enjoy."

Serving: 4 | Prep: 40 m | Cook: 15 m | Ready in: 55 m

Ingredients

- 1 red bell pepper
- salt and black pepper to taste
- 1/2 cup olive oil
- 4 portobello mushroom caps, cleaned
- 4 slices onion
- 4 Kaiser rolls, split
- 4 teaspoons mayonnaise
- 1 teaspoon roasted garlic, mashed into a paste (optional)
- 4 ounces buffalo mozzarella, thinly sliced
- 4 slices tomato
- 16 fresh basil leaves, divided

Direction

- Preheat an outdoor grill for medium-high heat, and lightly oil the grate.
- Place the red bell pepper onto the preheated grill, and grill until the skin is completely charred on all sides, 10 to 15 minutes. Place the pepper into a paper bag, seal the bag, and let the pepper cool. When cooled, remove the charred skin, slice the

- pepper into quarters, and remove the seeds. Thinly slice the pepper and set aside.
- Mix salt and pepper into the olive oil in a small bowl. Brush the smooth side of the mushrooms with the seasoned oil, and grill, oiled side down, until the mushrooms show grill marks, about 3 minutes. Brush the gill sides of the mushrooms with more seasoned olive oil, flip the mushrooms, and grill until the mushrooms are softened and juicy, about 3 more minutes. Set the mushrooms aside and keep warm.
- Lightly grill the slices of onion until softened and lightly browned, about 2 minutes per side. Spread the rolls out onto the grill to toast, about 1 minute. Mix the mayonnaise and roasted garlic in a bowl.
- Spread each roll with garlic mayonnaise, and make each sandwich with 1 mushroom cap, 1 ounce sliced mozzarella cheese, 1 slice of tomato, 4 basil leaves, 1 slice of grilled onion, and 1/4 the roasted red pepper slices. Repeat for remaining sandwiches.

Nutrition Information

- Calories: 520 calories
- Total Fat: 38.8 g
- Cholesterol: 24 mg
- Sodium: 295 mg
- Total Carbohydrate: 32 g
- Protein: 12.7 g

51. Grilled Portobello with Basil Mayonnaise Sandwich

"A light vegetarian sandwich with great flavor that is perfect for summer. You can use just about any type of bread but Kaiser rolls or burger buns are best. I like to serve this with grilled squash and a glass of white wine!"

Serving: 6 | Prep: 10 m | Cook: 10 m | Ready in: 25 m

Ingredients

- 1/3 cup balsamic vinegar
- 1/4 cup olive oil
- 1 tablespoon minced garlic
- 6 portobello mushroom caps
- 1/2 cup mayonnaise
- 1 tablespoon Dijon mustard
- 1 teaspoon lemon juice
- 2 tablespoons chopped fresh basil
- 6 kaiser rolls, split, toasted
- 1 tablespoon butter
- 6 leaves lettuce
- 6 tomato slices

Direction

- Preheat an outdoor grill for medium heat, and lightly oil the grate. Whisk together the balsamic vinegar, olive oil, and garlic in a small bowl.
- Arrange the portobello mushrooms gill-side up on a tray or baking sheet. Brush the mushrooms with some of the vinegar mixture, and allow to marinate for 3 to 5 minutes.

- Place the marinated mushrooms on the preheated grill, gill-side down. Grill mushrooms until tender, brushing both sides of the mushrooms with the remaining marinade, about 4 minutes on each side.
- Mix the mayonnaise, dijon mustard, lemon juice, and basil in a small bowl. Butter the toasted kaiser rolls, then spread with the mayonnaise mixture. Divide the mushrooms, lettuce, and tomato slices evenly to make 6 sandwiches.

Nutrition Information

- Calories: 412 calories
- Total Fat: 27.7 g
- Cholesterol: 12 mg
- Sodium: 417 mg
- Total Carbohydrate: 35.6 g
- Protein: 8.3 g

52. Grilled Portobellos Sauteed in Wine

"This recipe is a great addition to beef roast or a grilled steak. It is easy, quick, and can be prepared in the time it takes the steak to be grilled, if need be. We were absolutely amazed when this recipe became a favorite of our 2 year old grand daughter!"

Serving: 4

Ingredients

- 4 portobello mushroom caps
- 1 tablespoon olive oil
- 1 tablespoon butter
- 1 shallot, thinly sliced
- 1 cup white wine

Direction

- Preheat grill for high heat.
- Place mushrooms onto the grill, smooth side up. Grill until they start to soften, about 10 minutes. Turn over, and grill on the other side for about 5 minutes.
- Meanwhile, heat olive oil and butter in a large skillet over medium heat. Add the shallot, and fry for a few minutes, stirring frequently.
- Remove mushrooms to a cutting board, and slice. Place into the skillet, and increase the heat to high. Cook for about a minute, then pour in the wine. Continue to cook and stir until the wine is nearly evaporated. Remove from heat, and serve.

Nutrition Information

- Calories: 145 calories
- Total Fat: 6.5 g
- Cholesterol: 8 mg
- Sodium: 32 mg
- Total Carbohydrate: 9.4 g
- Protein: 3.2 g

53. Grilled Steak and Vegetable Salad from Publix

"Make a dish with savory steak on a bed of greens and tender grilled veggies, all topped with a white balsamic glaze."

Serving: 4 | Prep: 30 m | Ready in: 30 m

Ingredients

- 1 1/2 pounds grilling steaks (strip, rib eye, tenderloin)
- 1 teaspoon kosher salt, divided
- 1/2 teaspoon ground black pepper
- 1 medium zucchini, halved lengthwise
- 3 plum (Roma) tomatoes, halved
- 1 (6 ounce) package fresh sliced portobello mushrooms, stems and gills removed
- 2 tablespoons olive oil
- 8 tablespoons balsamic glaze (reduced balsamic vinegar), divided
- 1 (5 ounce) bag mixed salad greens with arugula
- 4 tablespoons Caesar salad dressing, divided

Direction

- Preheat grill (or grill pan).
- Season steaks with 1/2 teaspoon salt and pepper. Place steaks on grill (or in grill pan); grill 3-4 minutes on each side or until steak internal temperature is 145 degrees F. Remove steaks from grill; let stand 5 minutes before slicing.

- Combine zucchini, tomatoes, portobellos, oil, and remaining 1/2 teaspoon salt. Place vegetables on grill; grill 2-3 minutes on each side or until tender and grill marks begin to show.
- Remove vegetables from grill; cut into bite-size pieces. Slice steaks.
- Divide salad greens onto 4 serving plates; top with vegetables and steak. Drizzle each salad with balsamic glaze and salad dressing. Serve.

Nutrition Information

- Calories: 385 calories
- Total Fat: 25.1 g
- Cholesterol: 99 mg
- Sodium: 683 mg
- Total Carbohydrate: 15.3 g
- Protein: 22.9 g

54. Grilled Stuffed Portobello Mushroom Caps

"Large portobello mushroom caps, grilled with a creamy herb and garlic sauce, grape tomatoes, and cheese, make a delicious main course and can be served atop torn salad greens for a complete meal."

Serving: 4 | Prep: 25 m | Ready in: 25 m

Ingredients

- 4 large portobello mushrooms
- 2 teaspoons olive oil
- 1/2 cup PHILADELPHIA Herb Garlic Cooking Creme
- 1/2 cup grape tomatoes, quartered
- 2 tablespoons Kraft 100% Parmesan Shredded Cheese
- 1 green onion, thinly sliced

Direction

- Heat barbecue to medium heat.
- Discard stems from mushrooms; scrape out gills with small spoon. Brush mushrooms with oil; grill 2 min. on each side or just until mushrooms start to soften. Place, rounded-sides down, on foil-covered baking sheet. Dab insides of caps with paper towels to remove excess moisture.
- Fill caps with remaining ingredients.
- Grill 6 to 8 min. or until filling is heated through. Serve warm.

Nutrition Information

- Calories: 103 calories
- Total Fat: 8 g
- Cholesterol: 20 mg
- Sodium: 316 mg
- Total Carbohydrate: 4.1 g
- Protein: 4.3 g

55. Grilled Tequila Portobello

"Succulent moist portobello mushrooms do a fiesta of flavor dances sure to enhance any entree."

Serving: 2 | Prep: 5 m | Cook: 10 m | Ready in: 45 m

Ingredients

- 1/4 cup tequila
- 1/8 cup unsalted butter, melted
- 2 tablespoons roasted garlic oil
- 1 lime, juiced
- 3 cloves garlic, minced
- 1 large portobello mushroom, cut into 3/4 inch slices

Direction

- In a small bowl, mix together tequila, melted butter, roasted garlic oil, lime juice, and minced garlic. Let stand for at least 15 minutes.
- Preheat grill for medium heat.
- Brush grate with vegetable oil. Brush mushroom slices with tequila mixture, and place on grill. Cook until the mushroom slices begin to wilt, then turn and brush with more of the tequila mixture. Cook for a few minutes, until mushrooms are tender. Watch carefully so they do not burn.

Nutrition Information

- Calories: 314 calories
- Total Fat: 25.3 g

- Cholesterol: 31 mg
- Sodium: 6 mg
- Total Carbohydrate: 5.9 g
- Protein: 1.9 g

56. Grilled VeggiePortobello Mushroom Burgers

"Portobello mushrooms, winter squash, and eggplant are marinated, then grilled and topped with blue cheese in what's become a favorite at my house."

Serving: 6 | Prep: 20 m | Cook: 6 m | Ready in: 2 h 26 m

Ingredients

- 6 large portobello mushroom, stems removed
- 1 eggplant, sliced into 1/2 inch rounds
- 1 medium yellow squash, cut into 1/4-inch slices
- 1 zucchini, cut into 1/4-inch slices
- 1 (16 fl oz) bottle balsamic vinaigrette
- 1 (4 ounce) package crumbled blue cheese
- 6 hamburger buns, split and lightly toasted

Direction

- Place the mushrooms, eggplant, winter squash, and zucchini into a shallow bowl or baking dish. Drizzle with the balsamic vinaigrette, turning to coat evenly. Cover, and refrigerate at least 2 hours, or up to 24 hours, stirring occasionally.
- Preheat grill to medium-high heat.
- Drain vegetables and discard marinade. Place vegetables on preheated grill, and cook until lightly browned, turning once, or about 3 minutes on each side. (Note that cooking times vary between grills.) Sprinkle the mushrooms with blue cheese, and let the cheese melt slightly.

- Open the 6 hamburger buns and divide the eggplant, squash, and zucchini among bottom halves. Place the portobello mushrooms on top of the vegetables, cheese side up. Top with the remaining 6 hamburger bun halves. If necessary, use toothpicks to hold the buns in place. Serve immediately.

Nutrition Information

- Calories: 491 calories
- Total Fat: 32.1 g
- Cholesterol: 14 mg
- Sodium: 1448 mg
- Total Carbohydrate: 43.1 g
- Protein: 12 g

57. Grilled Zucchini with Portobello and Goat Cheese

"I was itching to do a recipe with mushrooms and goat cheese, and this is what I came up with. It works as an entree or a side dish, and can be served alongside other grilled recipes. Using an outdoor grill will shorten the total prep time."

Serving: 4 | Prep: 25 m | Cook: 23 m | Ready in: 58 m

Ingredients

- 1/2 cup garlic and herb marinade
- 2 zucchini, halved lengthwise
- 2 gold zucchini, halved lengthwise
- 2 portobello mushroom caps
- 1/4 cup pine nuts
- 1 tablespoon olive oil
- 1 large shallot, diced
- 2 plum tomatoes, chopped
- 10 leaves basil, chopped
- 3 ounces goat cheese
- 1 tablespoon chopped fresh chives

Direction

- Preheat grill for medium heat and lightly oil the grate.
- Pour marinade into a shallow bowl. Add zucchini, gold zucchini, and mushrooms. Let marinate, flipping occasionally, 10 to 15 minutes.
- Grill zucchini and gold zucchini, turning occasionally and brushing with marinade, until golden brown, about 5 minutes. Repeat with mushrooms. Transfer to a serving plate.

- Place pine nuts in a small skillet over medium-low heat. Toast, tossing occasionally, until golden, 3 to 5 minutes.
- Set oven rack about 6 inches from the heat source and preheat the oven's broiler.
- Heat oil in a large oven-safe skillet. Add shallot; cook and stir until golden brown, about 2 minutes. Stir in tomatoes and basil; cook until softened, about 5 minutes. Remove from heat; add grilled zucchini, gold zucchini, and mushrooms. Coat with goat cheese.
- Transfer skillet to the preheated oven; broil, keeping oven door open, until goat cheese is golden brown, 3 to 5 minutes.
- Sprinkle toasted pine nuts and chives over goat cheese.

Nutrition Information

- Calories: 207 calories
- Total Fat: 14.4 g
- Cholesterol: 17 mg
- Sodium: 601 mg
- Total Carbohydrate: 12.7 g
- Protein: 9.1 g

58. Grits a Ya Ya

"A friend of mine made this for a Mardi Gras dinner. It was so delicious, I just had to have the recipe."

Serving: 6 | Prep: 20 m | Cook: 30 m | Ready in: 50 m

Ingredients

- 3 1/2 cups chicken stock
- 3/4 cup old fashioned grits
- 1/4 cup heavy cream, plus more as needed
- 1 cup shredded smoked Gouda cheese, or more to taste
- 1/4 cup butter
- 8 slices bacon, chopped
- 3 tablespoons butter
- 1 tablespoon minced shallot
- 1 tablespoon minced garlic
- 1 splash white wine
- 1 pound jumbo shrimp, peeled and deveined
- 2 cups chopped spinach
- 1 cup chopped portobello mushrooms
- 1/4 cup sliced green onions
- 2 cups heavy cream
- 1 dash hot pepper sauce, or to taste
- salt and ground black pepper to taste

Direction

- Bring the chicken stock to a boil in a saucepan over high heat.
- Slowly pour the grits into the stock while stirring constantly.

- Reduce heat to low; simmer until the grits are tender and thick, 15 to 20 minutes, stirring occasionally.
- Stir in 1/4 cup heavy cream to thin the grits.
- Stir in the Gouda cheese and 1/4 cup butter until melted and smooth.
- While the grits are cooking, place the bacon in a large, deep skillet over medium heat; cook until the bacon fat is rendered, about 3 minutes.
- Stir in the shallot and garlic; cooking and stirring until the shallots are tender, about 5 minutes.
- Pour in the white wine and stir in 3 tablespoons butter, cooking and stirring until the butter has melted.
- Drop the shrimp in the skillet; cook and stir until they are bright pink on the outside and the meat is no longer transparent in the center, about 3 minutes.
- Stir in the spinach, mushrooms, and green onions; cook and stir until the spinach wilts, about 2 minutes more.
- Remove the shrimp with a slotted spoon.
- Stir in 2 cups heavy cream. Simmer until the cream is reduced by about a third, about 10 minutes.
- Season with hot sauce, salt, and pepper.
- Return the shrimp to the skillet to heat through.
- Serve shrimp and sauce over the prepared grits.

Nutrition Information

- Calories: 839 calories
- Total Fat: 70.5 g
- Cholesterol: 322 mg
- Sodium: 1083 mg
- Total Carbohydrate: 21.8 g
- Protein: 29.6 g

59. Gunnar and Ravens Burgundy Sauce

"Great with outdoor-grilled steaks! My son and I came up with this recipe over Memorial Day Weekend, 2005. The whole family loved it!"

Serving: 8 | Prep: 10 m | Cook: 15 m | Ready in: 25 m

Ingredients

- 1 tablespoon butter
- 1 tablespoon olive oil
- 2/3 cup chopped onion
- 2 cloves garlic, chopped
- 2 tablespoons all-purpose flour
- 2/3 cup beef broth
- 1 cup Burgundy wine
- 1 pinch dried basil, or to taste
- 1 pinch dried oregano, or to taste
- 1 1/2 cups sliced baby portobello mushrooms

Direction

- Heat butter and olive oil in a large skillet over low heat; cook and stir onion and garlic in the hot butter-oil mixture until onion is transparent, 5 to 10 minutes. Add flour and slowly pour in beef broth while stirring constantly until flour is smoothly mixed into the broth and vegetables.
- Stir Burgundy wine into onion-flour mixture; season with basil and oregano. Bring mixture to a simmer; add mushrooms. Cook and stir until sauce is thickened, about 10 minutes.

Nutrition Information

- Calories: 74 calories
- Total Fat: 3.3 g
- Cholesterol: 4 mg
- Sodium: 79 mg
- Total Carbohydrate: 4.9 g
- Protein: 1.2 g

60. Hot and Sour Tofu Soup Suan La Dofu Tang

"Forget the complicated Cantonese Hot and Sour Soup with a million ingredients! This is an authentic central Chinese version that will warm your heart and your palate without sending you on a hunt for ingredients."

Serving: 2 | Prep: 15 m | Cook: 10 m | Ready in: 25 m

Ingredients

- 4 cups vegetable broth
- 1 (12 ounce) package silken tofu, diced
- 2 green onions, chopped
- 1 eggs, beaten
- 1 portobello mushroom, halved and sliced
- 2 cups chopped cabbage
- 1 tablespoon Thai chile sauce
- 1 tablespoon rice vinegar
- 3 tablespoons soy sauce
- 1 teaspoon citric acid powder (optional)

Direction

- Measure broth into a saucepan, and bring to a simmer over medium-low heat. Add tofu and green onions. Slowly drizzle in the beaten egg to make long strands of egg. Add mushrooms and cabbage, and simmer for 5 minutes. Remove from heat, and season with chili sauce, vinegar and soy sauce. Stir in citric acid if using.

Nutrition Information

- Calories: 256 calories
- Total Fat: 8.3 g
- Cholesterol: 93 mg
- Sodium: 2390 mg
- Total Carbohydrate: 25.5 g
- Protein: 21.2 g

61. Hot Portobello Mushroom Sandwich

"Even my husband likes this flavorful mushroom sandwich."

Serving: 1 | Prep: 10 m | Cook: 5 m | Ready in: 15 m

Ingredients

- 1 portobello mushroom cap, cut into 1/2-inch slices
- 1 tablespoon red wine vinegar
- 2 slices pumpernickel rye bread
- 1 tablespoon Dijon mustard
- 1 tablespoon sliced pimento-stuffed green olives
- 2 slices Havarti cheese

Direction

- Preheat oven to 400 degrees F (200 degrees C).
- Place mushroom slices in a bowl. Sprinkle mushrooms with red wine vinegar. Lay the bread slices on a baking sheet. Spread mustard evenly on one slice. Arrange the mushroom slices on the slice of bread with the mustard. Place the green olive slices on the other slice of bread. Cover each piece of bread with the Havarti cheese.
- Bake in preheated oven until the cheese melts, 5 to 7 minutes. Remove from oven and put the slices together to make a sandwich.

Nutrition Information

- Calories: 467 calories
- Total Fat: 26.1 g
- Cholesterol: 71 mg
- Sodium: 1587 mg
- Total Carbohydrate: 40.5 g
- Protein: 20.7 g

62. HummusStuffed Portobello Caps

"This is a great party dish or appetizer, made with creamy hummus and bell pepper."

Serving: 6 | Prep: 15 m | Cook: 21 m | Ready in: 36 m

Ingredients

- 2 tablespoons olive oil
- 6 small portobello mushroom caps, stems and ribs removed
- 1/2 cup cream cheese, softened
- 1/2 green bell pepper, diced
- 3/4 cup roasted red pepper hummus
- salt and pepper to taste
- 1 teaspoon lemon pepper seasoning

Direction

- Preheat oven to 375 degrees F (190 degrees C).
- Heat olive oil in a large skillet over medium-high heat. Sear the portobello mushrooms for 3 minutes on each side until browned.
- Stir together cream cheese, green pepper, and hummus until evenly blended. Season the mushroom caps with salt and pepper on each side. Place the mushrooms onto a baking sheet, with the stem-side facing up. Sprinkle with lemon pepper, then fill with hummus mixture.
- Bake in preheated oven for 15 minutes until the filling is hot.

Nutrition Information

- Calories: 198 calories
- Total Fat: 15 g
- Cholesterol: 21 mg
- Sodium: 425 mg
- Total Carbohydrate: 12.6 g
- Protein: 5.5 g

63. Individual Grilled Veggie Pizzas

"Enjoy these easy gourmet individual pizzas prepared on the grill. They're good for entertaining or just for yourself."

Serving: 2 | Prep: 25 m | Cook: 14 m | Ready in: 39 m

Ingredients

- 1 large portobello mushroom, sliced
- 1 small zucchini, sliced
- 1/4 pound butternut squash - peeled, seeded, and thinly sliced
- 1 cup bite-size broccoli florets
- 1/4 cup chopped red onion
- 1 tablespoon olive oil
- 2 ounces refrigerated pizza crust
- 1/4 cup pesto
- 1/4 cup crumbled Gorgonzola or blue cheese
- 1/4 cup fontina cheese, cubed

Direction

- Preheat an outdoor grill for high heat.
- Place the mushrooms, zucchini, squash, broccoli, and onion in a grill pan, and brush with 2 tablespoons olive oil. Cook on preheated, covered grill until tender when pierced with a fork, about 5 minutes. Remove from grill and set aside.
- Roll out pizza dough on a floured surface to make two 8 inch circles 1/4 inch thick. Place onto pizza pans. Brush tops with remaining 1 tablespoon olive oil.

- Bake on preheated, covered grill until browned, turning once, about 3 minutes each side. Remove from grill and spread with pesto. Top with cooked vegetables. Sprinkle with blue and fontina cheeses. Return to grill, cover, and cook until cheese melts, about 3 minutes.

Nutrition Information

- Calories: 486 calories
- Total Fat: 33.4 g
- Cholesterol: 52 mg
- Sodium: 790 mg
- Total Carbohydrate: 29 g
- Protein: 19.5 g

64. Instant Pot Bison Pasta Pasta Bisonte

"A savory one-pot Instant Pot® adaptation of my pasta with bison and veggies recipe. Top with chopped basil and shaved Parmesan, if desired."

Serving: 6 | Prep: 15 m | Cook: 21 m | Ready in: 41 m

Ingredients

- 12 ounces ground bison
- 1 1/2 cups diced onion
- 1 1/2 cups diced red bell pepper
- 2 tablespoons olive oil
- 1 (8 ounce) package sliced baby portobello mushrooms
- 1/2 cup chopped fresh basil
- 4 cloves garlic, chopped
- 1 tablespoon dried oregano
- 1 bay leaf
- 2 (14.5 ounce) cans diced tomatoes
- 1 cup water
- 1/2 cup red wine
- 1 tablespoon tomato paste
- 1 (16 ounce) package trottole pasta
- 1/2 teaspoon salt
- 1/2 teaspoon onion powder
- 1/2 teaspoon garlic powder

Direction

- Turn on a multi-functional pressure cooker (such as Instant Pot(R)) and select Sauté function; heat until indicator reads 'Hot.' Add bison, onion, red bell pepper, and olive oil. Sauté until bison is browned and crumbly, 5 to 7 minutes. Add mushrooms; sauté until slightly softened, 1 to 2 minutes.
- Stir basil, garlic, oregano, and bay leaf into the bison mixture. Add tomatoes, water, wine, and tomato paste. Turn cooker off. Add pasta; stir until coated. Mix in salt, onion powder, and garlic powder.
- Set cooker to Manual. Close and lock the lid. Select high pressure according to manufacturer's instructions; set timer for 5 minutes. Allow 10 to 15 minutes for pressure to build.
- Release pressure carefully using the quick-release method according to manufacturer's instructions, about 5 minutes. Unlock and remove lid. Stir well.

Nutrition Information

- Calories: 459 calories
- Total Fat: 6.8 g
- Cholesterol: 29 mg
- Sodium: 460 mg
- Total Carbohydrate: 70.7 g
- Protein: 23.2 g

65. Instant Pot Butternut Squash Risotto with Mushrooms

"Easiest, no-fuss risotto in the Instant Pot®."

Serving: 6 | Prep: 10 m | Cook: 35 m | Ready in: 50 m

Ingredients

- 2 tablespoons olive oil
- 1 medium white onion, chopped
- 4 cups peeled and cubed butternut squash (1/2-inch pieces), divided
- 3 cloves garlic
- 2 cups Arborio rice
- 1/4 cup dry white wine
- 2 cups vegetable broth
- 1 (8 ounce) package sliced portobello mushrooms
- 1/2 cup chopped red bell pepper
- 1/2 teaspoon kosher salt
- 1/4 teaspoon freshly grated nutmeg
- 2 tablespoons chopped fresh flat-leaf parsley, or to taste
- 1/4 cup grated Parmesan cheese

Direction

- Turn on a multi-functional pressure cooker (such as Instant Pot(R)) and select Sauté function. Add olive oil when the pot is hot. Add onion; sauté, stirring occasionally, until translucent, about 5 minutes. Add 1/2 the butternut squash and the garlic.

Sauté, stirring occasionally, until squash is browned on all sides, 5 to 10 minutes.
- Push squash mixture to the side of the pot. Add rice and stir to coat. Sauté, stirring frequently, until starting to stick to the bottom of the pot, 3 to 4 minutes. Pour wine into the pot and bring to a boil while scraping the browned bits off the bottom with a wooden spoon.
- Pour vegetable broth, mushrooms, red bell pepper, salt, nutmeg, and the rest of the squash into the pot. Stir; close and lock the lid. Select high pressure according to manufacturer's instructions; set timer for 5 minutes. Allow 10 to 15 minutes for pressure to build.
- Cover vent with a towel and twist to release pressure using the quick-release method, about 5 minutes. Unlock and remove the lid. Stir in parsley and top with Parmesan cheese.

Nutrition Information

- Calories: 409 calories
- Total Fat: 5.9 g
- Cholesterol: 3 mg
- Sodium: 373 mg
- Total Carbohydrate: 78.8 g
- Protein: 9 g

66. Jims BeerBattered Portobello Mushrooms

"If you like portobello mushrooms and like them deep-fried, this is for you! Delicious! Serve with a chipotle-aioli sauce for dipping."

Serving: 4 | Prep: 15 m | Cook: 15 m | Ready in: 30 m

Ingredients

- oil for frying
- 2 cups bitter ale (such as Goose Island Honkers Ale®)
- 1 3/4 cups all-purpose flour
- 1/2 cup sesame seeds
- 2 tablespoons cornstarch
- 1 tablespoon baking powder
- 3 large portobello mushroom caps, cut into 1/2-inch slices

Direction

- Heat oil in a deep-fryer or large saucepan to 375 degrees F (190 degrees C).
- Whisk ale, flour, sesame seeds, cornstarch, and baking powder in a large bowl. The batter will be thick and slightly lumpy.
- Dip 7 to 8 strips of mushroom at a time into the batter, shaking off excess.
- Fry mushrooms in batches in the preheated oil until golden brown, 5 to 6 minutes.

Nutrition Information

- Calories: 574 calories
- Total Fat: 31.5 g
- Cholesterol: 0 mg
- Sodium: 257 mg
- Total Carbohydrate: 54.6 g
- Protein: 9.7 g

67. Kapusta

"Kapusta is a great side dish at any meal and even makes a great main dish for vegetarians. This recipe was passed down by my Polish grandmother. I grew up with it at every holiday meal and just love it. Sauerkraut takes on a whole new flavor when baked and is really delicious! Try it and see for yourself!"

Serving: 6 | Prep: 20 m | Cook: 1 h 10 m | Ready in: 1 h 30 m

Ingredients

- 6 tablespoons butter, divided
- 2 onions, chopped
- 1 large portobello mushrooms, sliced
- 1 1/2 cups sliced mushrooms
- 1/4 medium head cabbage, thinly sliced
- 1 (32 ounce) jar sauerkraut, drained and pressed
- 1/2 teaspoon white sugar
- 1/2 teaspoon dried thyme
- salt and pepper to taste

Direction

- Preheat oven to 350 degrees F (175 degrees C).
- Heat 4 tablespoons of butter over medium heat; sauté onions and mushrooms until tender.
- In a medium saucepan over high heat, boil cabbage for 10 minutes.
- In a 9 x 13 inch baking dish combine onions, mushrooms, cabbage, sauerkraut, sugar, thyme, salt and pepper; mix well. Dot remaining 2 tablespoons butter on top. Cover.
- Bake in preheated oven for 1 hour, stirring every 20 minutes.

Nutrition Information

- Calories: 151 calories
- Total Fat: 11.8 g
- Cholesterol: 31 mg
- Sodium: 760 mg
- Total Carbohydrate: 11 g
- Protein: 2.6 g

68. Kickin Portobello Dressing

"Thanksgiving dressing is made special with portobello mushrooms, caramelized onions, bacon and cranberries."

Serving: 12 | Prep: 40 m | Cook: 45 m | Ready in: 1 h 25 m

Ingredients

- 1 (1 pound) loaf French bread, cubed
- 1 (8 ounce) loaf Italian bread, cubed
- 1 pound sliced bacon, diced
- 3 sweet onions, chopped
- 2 1/4 cups chicken stock
- 12 ounces portobello mushroom caps, chopped
- 4 stalks celery with leaves, chopped
- 1/4 cup dried cranberries
- 1/4 cup raisins
- 1/4 cup golden raisins
- 2 teaspoons dried sage
- 1 teaspoon dried rosemary
- 3 eggs, beaten
- 1 teaspoon ground black pepper
- 2 teaspoons salt
- 1 cup butter, melted (optional)

Direction

- Preheat the oven to 250 degrees F (120 degrees C). Spread the bread cubes out in a single layer on rimmed baking sheets. Toast in the oven for 20 minutes, or until dry. Cool, and transfer to a large bowl.

- Fry the bacon pieces in a large skillet over medium heat until crisp. Remove from the pan to drain on paper towels. Add onions to the pan with the bacon grease: cook and stir over medium heat until starting to turn deep brown, about 15 minutes.
- Pour in 1/4 cup of the chicken stock, stirring to remove any bits that are stuck to the bottom of the skillet. Add the celery and mushrooms and season with sage, rosemary, salt and pepper. Drizzle this over the bread cubes, and toss to coat.
- Pour the rest of the chicken broth over the bread and add the bacon, cranberries, raisins and golden raisins. The stuffing can be made up to this point up to 3 days in advance.
- Preheat the oven to 350 degrees F (175 degrees C). Whisk the salt and pepper in with the eggs and stir into the bread cubes. Transfer to a disposable roasting pan, or a large baking dish. Drizzle melted butter over the top and cover with aluminum foil. If stuffing a turkey, mix in the eggs and melted butter; stuff in to the cavity right before roasting.
- Bake for 30 minutes in the preheated oven, then remove the aluminum foil and continue to bake for an additional 10 to 15 minutes, until the top is browned.

Nutrition Information

- Calories: 432 calories
- Total Fat: 23.4 g
- Cholesterol: 101 mg
- Sodium: 1299 mg
- Total Carbohydrate: 43.2 g
- Protein: 13.9 g

69. Kohlrabi Kale Mushroom and Bean Saute

"This is a great dish for those with a CSA who want new ways to cook with kale or kohlrabi."

Serving: 2 | Prep: 15 m | Cook: 10 m | Ready in: 25 m

Ingredients

- 2 tablespoons extra-virgin olive oil
- 2 cloves garlic, minced
- 1/4 teaspoon red pepper flakes
- 1 bunch kale, stemmed and coarsely chopped
- 1 cup chicken broth
- 2 kohlrabi - peeled, halved, and sliced
- 1 (15 ounce) can cannellini beans, drained and rinsed
- 12 ounces baby portobello mushrooms, sliced
- salt and ground black pepper to taste

Direction

- Heat oil in a 12-inch sauté pan over medium-high heat. Add garlic and red pepper flakes; sauté until fragrant, about 30 seconds. Add kale to the pan and toss.
- Pour in broth and reduce heat to medium. Add kohlrabi, cover, and cook until tender, 5 to 7 minutes.
- Add beans and mushrooms to the pan. Increase heat to medium-high and cook until excess liquid has evaporated and mushrooms are tender, 5 to 7 minutes more. Season with salt and pepper.

Nutrition Information

- Calories: 492 calories
- Total Fat: 16.7 g
- Cholesterol: 3 mg
- Sodium: 1231 mg
- Total Carbohydrate: 70.6 g
- Protein: 22.9 g

70. Leek Potato Mushroom Cheddar Soup

"Creamy and flavorful. Just add some croutons and it is simply delicious. We put together some of our favorite things in one pot to make this soup."

Serving: 6 | Prep: 30 m | Cook: 1 h 15 m | Ready in: 1 h 45 m

Ingredients

- 2 leeks, finely chopped (white part only)
- 1 clove garlic, finely chopped
- 4 medium potatoes (red or Yukon Gold), chopped
- 2 tablespoons butter, divided
- 1 tablespoon olive oil
- 1 1/2 teaspoons ground mustard
- 2 tablespoons flour
- 1/2 cup water
- 3 cups chicken broth
- salt, pepper, and celery salt, to taste
- 1/2 cup shredded Cheddar cheese
- 2 tablespoons Parmesan cheese
- 1 cup milk
- 3 ounces chopped portobello mushrooms
- croutons for garnish, if desired

Direction

- In a skillet, cook leek, garlic, and potato in 1 tablespoon of butter and the olive oil over medium low heat, stirring often. Do not allow potato to brown.

- Place mustard, salt, pepper, celery salt, and flour together in a bowl. Gradually whisk in water and chicken broth until well blended. Stir into potato mixture, and bring to a boil. Reduce to a simmer, and cook for 1 hour.
- Mash softened potatoes by hand so they remain lumpy. Stir in Cheddar and Parmesan cheeses until melted, then add milk but do not boil. Cook mushrooms over medium high heat in remaining 1 tablespoon of butter until soft. Add to the soup, and stir. Serve immediately with croutons, if desired.

Nutrition Information

- Calories: 289 calories
- Total Fat: 12.2 g
- Cholesterol: 25 mg
- Sodium: 909 mg
- Total Carbohydrate: 37.3 g
- Protein: 8.6 g

71. Linguine with Clam Sauce and Baby Portobello Mushrooms

"This is one of my all-time favorite meals. What makes the clam sauce so flavorful is the chicken bouillon, Worcestershire sauce, and baby portobello mushrooms. I recommend having this with some garlic bread and a nice glass of red wine. A very satisfying meal."

Serving: 4 | Prep: 15 m | Cook: 45 m | Ready in: 1 h

Ingredients

- 1 tablespoon olive oil
- 3 cloves garlic, chopped
- 1 (8 ounce) package baby portobello mushrooms, sliced and chopped
- 4 (6.5 ounce) cans chopped clams with juice
- 4 cubes chicken bouillon
- 1 tablespoon chopped fresh parsley
- 1 teaspoon dried basil
- 1 teaspoon dried oregano
- 1 tablespoon Worcestershire sauce
- 1 (16 ounce) package uncooked linguini pasta
- 1/2 cup butter

Direction

- Warm olive oil in a saucepan over medium heat. Stir in garlic and mushrooms; cook until mushrooms are tender. Stir in clam juice, chicken bouillon, parsley, basil, oregano, and Worcestershire sauce. Increase heat to high, and bring to a quick boil. Reduce heat to medium; simmer 30 minutes.

- Meanwhile, bring a large pot of lightly salted water to a boil. Add pasta, and cook until al dente, about 8-10 minutes. Drain and set aside.
- Stir chopped clams and butter into the sauce; simmer 15 minutes more. Pour over cooked pasta to serve.

Nutrition Information

- Calories: 941 calories
- Total Fat: 33 g
- Cholesterol: 185 mg
- Sodium: 1574 mg
- Total Carbohydrate: 97 g
- Protein: 64.7 g

72. Linguine with Portobello Mushrooms

"Portobello mushrooms are a really good meat substitute, especially when they are grilled. If possible, use fresh herbs in this recipe."

Serving: 8 | Prep: 15 m | Cook: 30 m | Ready in: 45 m

Ingredients

- 4 portobello mushroom caps
- 2 tablespoons extra virgin olive oil
- 1 pound linguine pasta
- 1 teaspoon red wine vinegar
- 1 teaspoon chopped fresh oregano
- 1 teaspoon chopped fresh basil
- 1/2 teaspoon chopped fresh rosemary
- 2 cloves garlic, peeled and crushed
- 2 teaspoons lemon juice
- salt and pepper to taste

Direction

- Preheat the oven broiler.
- Bring a large pot of lightly salted water to a boil. Add linguine, and cook for 9 to 13 minutes or until al dente; drain.
- Brush the mushrooms with 1/2 the olive oil, and arrange on a medium baking sheet. Broil in the prepared oven 6 to 8 minutes, turning frequently, until browned and tender.
- Cut the mushrooms into 1/4 inch slices, and place in a medium bowl. Mix with the remaining olive oil, red wine vinegar,

- oregano, basil, rosemary, garlic, and lemon juice. Season with salt and pepper.
- In a large bowl, toss together cooked linguine and the mushroom mixture.

Nutrition Information

- Calories: 250 calories
- Total Fat: 4.8 g
- Cholesterol: 0 mg
- Sodium: 152 mg
- Total Carbohydrate: 44.6 g
- Protein: 9 g

73. Mamitas Mojito Scallop Kabobs with Stuffed Tomatoes

"Fresh and large scallops stew in a marinade of tangy Cuban 'mojito.' Two large scallops meet chunks of yellow squash, zucchini, and portabello mushrooms on a stick to form a kabob. It's sure to take you away to the tropics in the middle of your work week. Serve with a baked and stuffed broccoli-cheese tomato."

Serving: 2 | Prep: 20 m | Cook: 35 m | Ready in: 8 h 55 m

Ingredients

- Mojito Marinade
- 1 cup orange juice
- 1/2 cup lemon juice
- 1 tablespoon salt
- 1 tablespoon onion powder
- 1 tablespoon garlic powder
- 1 teaspoon black pepper
- 1 teaspoon white sugar
- 8 large scallops
- 2 yellow squash, cut into 4 large chunks
- 2 zucchinis, cut into 4 large chunks
- 1 (8 ounce) package portobello mushroom caps, cut into large chunks
- 4 bamboo skewers, soaked in water for 60 minutes
- 1/2 cup fresh basil
- Stuffed Tomatoes
- 2 large tomatoes, cored
- 1 (12 ounce) package microwaveable broccoli in cheese sauce
- 1 1/2 cups cooked brown rice
- 1 slice American cheese, cut into 4 strips

Direction

- Whisk orange juice, lemon juice, salt, onion powder, garlic powder, black pepper, and sugar together in a large bowl to dissolve seasoning into the liquid. Add scallops, yellow squash, zucchinis, and portobello mushroom to the mojito marinade; toss to coat.
- Cover bowl with plastic wrap and refrigerate 8 hours to overnight.
- Preheat oven to 400 degrees F (200 degrees C).
- Thread onto a skewer a piece of mushroom, yellow squash, zucchini, and a scallop, respectively. Repeat so there are two of each item on the skewer; repeat with remaining skewers. Sprinkle fresh basil evenly over the skewers.
- Carefully remove tomato insides with a spoon; discard tomato insides.
- Pour broccoli with cheese sauce into a microwave-safe bowl; cook in microwave until broccoli is tender and the sauce is melted, 3 to 5 minutes.
- Stir broccoli with cheese sauce and rice together in a bowl; spoon into the hollowed-out tomatoes. Place 2 strips American cheese atop the mixture in a crossing pattern.
- Cook the skewers in preheated oven until the scallops are cooked through, 25 to 30 minutes. Remove from oven to a plate; cover with aluminum foil to keep warm.
- Reduce oven heat to 350 degrees F (175 degrees C).
- Bake tomatoes in the oven until the cheese is bubbling, 5 to 10 minutes. Serve with the skewers.

Nutrition Information

- Calories: 770 calories

- Total Fat: 20.7 g
- Cholesterol: 103 mg
- Sodium: 4379 mg
- Total Carbohydrate: 98.6 g
- Protein: 56.4 g

74. Marinated Portobello Mushrooms

"Portobello mushrooms marinated in balsamic vinegar and rosemary, then grilled - these are heaven. If you don't have a grill, they're also delicious fried in a skillet. Portobello mushrooms are extremely large, dark brown mushrooms that are simply the fully mature form of the crimini mushroom, a variation of the common white mushroom."

Serving: 4 | Prep: 5 m | Cook: 10 m | Ready in: 45 m

Ingredients

- 2 portobello mushrooms, cut into 1/2 inch pieces
- 10 tablespoons balsamic vinegar
- 4 tablespoons dried rosemary
- salt and pepper to taste
- 1 tablespoon olive oil

Direction

- In a nonporous glass dish or bowl, combine the mushrooms, vinegar, rosemary, and salt and pepper. Stir to coat. Cover, and refrigerate for at least 30 minutes.
- Preheat grill for high heat.
- Brush grate with oil, and arrange marinated mushrooms on hot grill. Turn after 2 to 3 minutes, and continue grilling until mushrooms are heated through and look wilted and black. Serve hot off the grill.

Nutrition Information

- Calories: 80 calories
- Total Fat: 4.1 g
- Cholesterol: 0 mg
- Sodium: 15 mg
- Total Carbohydrate: 10.7 g
- Protein: 1.7 g

75. Meatless Mushroom Tart

"This is a wonderful, savory, quiche-like pie that I use as a brunch entree and also as a vegetarian main dish to supplement my traditional Thanksgiving dinner for family and friends. It could also be altered for use as an appetizer if made using mini-tart pan. It always gets rave reviews!"

Serving: 8 | Prep: 25 m | Cook: 1 h 2 m | Ready in: 2 h 27 m

Ingredients

- 1 (17.25 ounce) package frozen puff pastry, thawed according to package instructions
- 3 tablespoons butter, melted
- 2 1/2 cups chopped yellow onion
- 8 cups portobello mushrooms, coarsely chopped
- 2 tablespoons fresh thyme leaves, finely chopped
- 1 (8 ounce) package cream cheese, cut into cubes, at room temperature
- salt and ground black pepper to taste
- 1 large egg yolk
- 1 tablespoon milk

Direction

- Preheat oven to 400 degrees F (200 degrees C). Lightly grease a baking sheet.
- Line a 10-inch pie dish with 1 sheet of puff pastry. Trim the edge so 1 inch hangs over the rim of the dish.
- Bake in preheated oven just long enough to set the pastry, 5 to 10 minutes.

- Cut the second sheet of puff pastry into 1 inch wide strips. Place the strips on the prepared baking sheet. Refrigerate the strips and the baked pie shell for at least 30 minutes, or up to 24 hours.
- Meanwhile, melt the butter in a skillet over medium-high heat. Stir in the onions, and cook until soft and transparent, about 6 minutes. Stir in the mushrooms and thyme, and cook until the mushrooms soften and release their juices, about 6 minutes. Mix the cream cheese into the mushroom mixture, stirring until melted. Season to taste with salt and pepper.
- Spoon the mushroom mixture into the pie shell. Arrange the pastry strips in a lattice pattern across the filling. Fold and crimp the ends of the strips together with the pie shell edge trimming any necessary pastry to make an even edge.
- Whisk the egg yolk and milk together in a small bowl, and use to brush the top of the pie.
- Bake in preheated oven until the crust is golden brown and the filling is heated through, up to 45 minutes. Check for doneness after 30 minutes. Cool another 30 minutes before serving.

Nutrition Information

- Calories: 523 calories
- Total Fat: 37.9 g
- Cholesterol: 68 mg
- Sodium: 274 mg
- Total Carbohydrate: 38 g
- Protein: 10 g

76. Megans Marvelous Mushrooms

"Megan's stuffed mushrooms."

Serving: 10 | Prep: 20 m | Cook: 10 m | Ready in: 30 m

Ingredients

- 1 (16 ounce) package baby portobello mushrooms
- 1/2 cup grated Parmesan cheese
- 1/4 cup shredded mozzarella cheese
- 3 green onions, finely chopped
- 1 tablespoon olive oil
- 1 clove garlic, finely chopped
- 1/2 teaspoon salt
- 1/2 teaspoon ground black pepper

Direction

- Preheat oven to 375 degrees F (190 degrees C). Grease a shallow 2-quart baking dish.
- Remove stems from mushrooms and finely chop stems. Combine chopped stems, Parmesan cheese, mozzarella cheese, green onions, olive oil, garlic, salt, and black pepper in a bowl. Spoon filling into mushroom caps; arrange caps in the prepared baking dish.
- Bake in the preheated oven until the mushrooms are tender, 10 to 15 minutes.

Nutrition Information

- Calories: 52 calories
- Total Fat: 3.2 g
- Cholesterol: 6 mg
- Sodium: 199 mg
- Total Carbohydrate: 3 g
- Protein: 3.4 g

77. Mushroom and Onion Vegetarian Tacos

"Vegetarians and meat-lovers will both love these delicious tacos. Mushrooms provide 'meaty' and filling flavor, balanced out by sweet caramelized onions."

Serving: 4 | Prep: 25 m | Ready in: 25 m

Ingredients

- Tacos:
- 1 tablespoon vegetable oil
- 1 medium red onion, sliced
- 3 large fresh portabella mushrooms, sliced, cut in half, stems removed
- 2 tablespoons Old El Paso® taco seasoning mix
- 2 tablespoons water
- 8 Old El Paso® flour tortillas for soft tacos fajitas
- Toppings, as desired:
- 1 cup guacamole
- 1/2 cup sour cream
- 1/2 cup crumbled queso fresco cheese

Direction

- In 12-inch nonstick skillet, heat oil over medium-high heat. Cook onion in oil, stirring occasionally, until brown. Add mushrooms. Cook 6 to 8 minutes or until tender. Reduce heat to low. Add taco seasoning mix and water. Cook about 5 minutes or until water is absorbed. Remove from heat.
- Spoon filling on tortillas. Add toppings. Roll up tortillas.

Nutrition Information

- Calories: 387 calories
- Total Fat: 22.6 g
- Cholesterol: 23 mg
- Sodium: 852 mg
- Total Carbohydrate: 38.5 g
- Protein: 9.8 g

78. Mushroom Cap Chorizo Burger

"You will not miss the bun with this extremely flavorful stuffed portobello mushroom cap chorizo burger. It is sure to impress even the pickiest eaters! Top with cheese if desired!"

Serving: 8 | Prep: 15 m | Cook: 27 m | Ready in: 42 m

Ingredients

- 8 large portobello mushrooms, stems removed
- 1 tablespoon vegetable oil, or more as needed
- salt and ground black pepper to taste
- 1 pound ground beef
- 1 pound chorizo sausage
- 1/2 onion, diced
- 4 slices cooked bacon, chopped
- 1 egg
- 2 cloves garlic, minced
- 1/4 cup chopped fresh cilantro
- 1/2 teaspoon salt
- 1/2 teaspoon ground black pepper
- 1/2 teaspoon garlic powder
- 1/2 teaspoon onion powder
- 1/2 teaspoon chili powder

Direction

- Preheat oven to 375 degrees F (190 degrees C).
- Scrape the gills out of each mushroom. Brush olive oil over each mushroom (top and bottom) and season with salt and pepper. Arrange mushrooms, gill-side up, on a baking sheet.

- Bake in the preheated oven until tender, about 7 minutes.
- Combine ground beef, chorizo, onion, bacon, egg, garlic, cilantro, 1/2 teaspoon salt, 1/2 teaspoon black pepper, garlic powder, onion powder, and chili powder in a large bowl just until mixed; shape into 8 patties. Place a patty on top of each mushroom.
- Bake in the preheated oven until burgers are fully cooked, about 20 minutes. An instant-read thermometer inserted into the center should read at least 160 degrees F (70 degrees C).

Nutrition Information

- Calories: 427 calories
- Total Fat: 34.2 g
- Cholesterol: 111 mg
- Sodium: 980 mg
- Total Carbohydrate: 3.2 g
- Protein: 25.2 g

79. Mushroom Kabobs

"This is a wonderful kabob for grilling. With more types of mushrooms available in the grocery store, you can now make these year-round using an assortment of button, portabello, shiitake, and crimini mushrooms."

Serving: 4 | Prep: 30 m | Cook: 10 m | Ready in: 40 m

Ingredients

- 3/4 cup sliced fresh mushrooms
- 2 red bell peppers, chopped
- 1 green bell pepper, cut into 1 inch pieces
- 1/4 cup olive oil
- 2 tablespoons lemon juice
- 1 clove garlic, minced
- 2 teaspoons chopped fresh thyme
- 1 teaspoon chopped fresh rosemary
- 1/4 teaspoon salt
- 1/4 teaspoon ground black pepper

Direction

- Preheat grill for medium heat.
- Thread mushrooms and peppers alternately on skewers.
- In a small bowl, mix together olive oil, lemon juice, garlic, thyme, rosemary, and salt and pepper. Brush mushrooms and peppers with this flavored oil.
- Brush grate with oil, and place kabobs on the grill. Baste frequently with oil mixture. Cook for about 4 to 6 minutes, or until mushrooms are tender and thoroughly cooked.

Nutrition Information

- Calories: 151 calories
- Total Fat: 13.8 g
- Cholesterol: 0 mg
- Sodium: 150 mg
- Total Carbohydrate: 6.5 g
- Protein: 1.4 g

80. Mushroom Lasagna with Garlic Parmesan Cream Sauce

"Yummy alternative to traditional lasagna."

Serving: 10 | Prep: 25 m | Cook: 1 h 17 m | Ready in: 1 h 42 m

Ingredients

- 1/2 (8 ounce) package lasagna noodles
- 1/4 cup butter, divided
- 6 large portobello mushroom caps, diced
- salt and ground black pepper to taste
- 1 large Vidalia onion, diced
- 5 cloves garlic, minced
- 2 cups whole milk
- 2 cups heavy whipping cream
- 3 cups grated Parmesan cheese
- 3 cups crumbled feta cheese
- 3 cups shredded mozzarella cheese

Direction

- Bring a large pot of lightly salted water to a boil. Cook lasagna noodles in the boiling water, stirring occasionally until tender yet firm to the bite, about 8 minutes. Drain.
- Melt 2 tablespoons butter in a large pot over medium heat. Cook and stir portobello mushrooms until soft, 5 to 10 minutes. Season lightly with salt and pepper.
- Melt remaining 2 tablespoons butter in a large pot over medium heat. Cook and stir onion and garlic in butter until deeply

browned, about 25 minutes. Pour in milk and heavy cream; bring to a simmer. Whisk in Parmesan cheese until sauce thickens slightly. Remove from heat; season lightly with salt and pepper.
- Preheat oven to 350 degrees F (175 degrees C).
- Layer lasagna noodles, portobello mushrooms, onion sauce, feta cheese, and mozzarella cheese in a baking dish, ending with cheese on top.
- Bake in the preheated oven until lasagna is heated through and lightly browned on top, about 30 minutes.

Nutrition Information

- Calories: 672 calories
- Total Fat: 52.4 g
- Cholesterol: 192 mg
- Sodium: 1508 mg
- Total Carbohydrate: 18.6 g
- Protein: 32.5 g

81. Mushroom Sliders

"Delicious burgers with all the health benefits and none of the sugar or gluten you find in normal buns."

Serving: 6 | Prep: 10 m | Cook: 15 m | Ready in: 25 m

Ingredients

- 1 pound lean ground beef, or more to taste
- 1 large egg
- 1 small onion, finely chopped
- 1 cup finely chopped mushrooms
- 1 teaspoon ground black pepper
- 1/2 teaspoon garlic salt
- salt to taste
- 6 portobello mushrooms, or more to taste
- 1 green bell pepper, halved and seeded
- 1 red bell pepper, halved and seeded
- 1 yellow bell pepper, halved and seeded

Direction

- Preheat an outdoor grill for medium-high heat and lightly oil the grate.
- Mix ground beef, egg, onion, and chopped mushrooms together in a bowl, seasoning with pepper, garlic salt, and salt as you mix. Form mixture into patties about 2 inches in diameter.
- Grill patties on the preheated grill until browned and desired doneness is reached, 5 to 7 minutes per side. An instant-read

thermometer inserted into the center should read at least 160 degrees F (70 degrees C).
- Grill portobello mushrooms, green bell pepper, red bell pepper, and yellow bell pepper on the grill until tender, 3 to 5 minutes per side. Use 2 mushrooms and as the 'bun' for the burgers.

Nutrition Information

- Calories: 214 calories
- Total Fat: 11.6 g
- Cholesterol: 77 mg
- Sodium: 240 mg
- Total Carbohydrate: 10.9 g
- Protein: 18.1 g

82. Mushroom Spinach Mac and Cheese

"Tofu adds a creamy texture to this healthy spin on Macaroni and Cheese! Great for a side dish or as a meal by itself. Top with bread crumbs, crushed crackers, or cereal before baking if desired."

Serving: 6 | Prep: 25 m | Cook: 50 m | Ready in: 1 h 15 m

Ingredients

- 1 (16 ounce) package elbow macaroni
- 1 (12 ounce) package soft silken tofu
- 8 ounces shredded Swiss cheese
- 1/2 cup Greek yogurt
- 1 teaspoon Dijon mustard
- 1 tablespoon olive oil
- 8 ounces portobello mushrooms, stemmed and sliced
- 1 cup frozen spinach, thawed
- 1 green bell pepper, chopped
- 1 onion, diced
- 2 cloves garlic, minced
- salt and ground black pepper to taste

Direction

- Bring a large pot of lightly salted water to a boil. Cook elbow macaroni in the boiling water, stirring occasionally until tender yet firm to the bite, 8 minutes. Drain and transfer to a 9x13-inch casserole dish.
- Preheat oven to 350 degrees F (175 degrees C).

- Blend tofu in a food processor until smooth, about 2 minutes. Add Swiss cheese, Greek yogurt, and Dijon mustard; mix well to combine.
- Heat oil in a large skillet over medium-high heat. Add mushrooms, spinach, green bell pepper, onion, and garlic; sauté until tender, about 5 minutes. Stir tofu mixture into the skillet. Cook until flavors combine, 2 to 3 minutes. Season with salt and ground black pepper.
- Spoon tofu and mushroom mixture over macaroni in the casserole dish; mix to combine. Cover with aluminum foil.
- Bake in the preheated oven until bubbly and golden, about 30 minutes.

Nutrition Information

- Calories: 524 calories
- Total Fat: 17.3 g
- Cholesterol: 39 mg
- Sodium: 160 mg
- Total Carbohydrate: 66.2 g
- Protein: 25.9 g

83. Nayzas Mushroom Fiesta Cups

"Portobello mushrooms are stuffed with refried beans and topped with Cheddar cheese and homemade corn salsa in these fun fiesta cups. This recipe was made in a Panasonic CIO and appears on an episode of the Dinner Spinner TV Show on The CW!"

Serving: 3 | Prep: 30 m | Cook: 15 m | Ready in: 45 m

Ingredients

- Corn Salsa:
- 1 (15 ounce) can corn, drained
- 3 tablespoons chopped fresh cilantro
- 2 limes, juiced
- 1/2 jalapeno pepper, chopped
- 2 tablespoons ground cumin
- 1 tablespoon onion powder
- 1 tablespoon dried oregano
- 1 1/2 teaspoons chopped garlic
- 1/2 teaspoon Himalayan salt
- 2 teaspoons olive oil
- 2 dashes liquid smoke flavoring
- 3 portobello mushrooms, stems removed
- 2 teaspoons ground cumin
- 2 teaspoons dried oregano
- 2 teaspoons garlic powder
- 2 teaspoons onion powder
- 1 teaspoon ground black pepper
- 1/2 teaspoon sea salt
- 1 (16 ounce) can refried black beans
- 1 tablespoon ground cumin
- 1 tablespoon dried oregano

- 1 tablespoon garlic powder
- 1 tablespoon onion powder
- 1 teaspoon ground black pepper
- 1/2 teaspoon salt
- 1/2 cup shredded Cheddar cheese
- 1 avocado, roughly chopped and slightly mashed
- 1 Roma tomato, diced

Direction

- Mix corn, cilantro, lime juice, jalapeno, 2 tablespoons cumin, 1 tablespoon onion powder, 1 tablespoon oregano, chopped garlic, and 1/2 teaspoon Himalayan salt together in a bowl until salsa is well mixed.
- Mix olive oil and liquid smoke together in a separate bowl; rub onto mushrooms. Season mushrooms with 2 teaspoons cumin, 2 teaspoons oregano, 2 teaspoons garlic powder, 2 teaspoons onion powder, 1 teaspoon black pepper, and 1/2 teaspoon sea salt. Place seasoned mushrooms onto a grill pan with the flat side down. (A grill pan for a countertop induction oven can also be used.)
- Place grill pan in the oven and heat oven to 445 degrees F (230 degrees C). (Or turn on a countertop induction oven to Combo 1.) Cook in the oven until tender, 9 to 10 minutes.
- Mix refried beans, 1 tablespoon cumin, 1 tablespoon oregano, 1 tablespoon garlic powder, 1 tablespoon onion powder, 1 teaspoon black pepper, and 1/2 teaspoon salt together in a saucepan over medium heat; cook and stir until heated through, about 5 minutes.
- Remove grill pan from oven and spoon bean mixture into mushrooms; top with Cheddar cheese.
- Return grill pan with mushrooms to oven. Set oven to broil and cook mushrooms until cheese is melted, 30 seconds to 1

minute.
- Spoon salsa over mushrooms and top with avocado and tomatoes.

Nutrition Information

- Calories: 459 calories
- Total Fat: 15.6 g
- Cholesterol: 32 mg
- Sodium: 2072 mg
- Total Carbohydrate: 68.2 g
- Protein: 20.9 g

84. Orzo and Chicken Stuffed Peppers

"This dish looks beautiful and tastes like you cooked all day. Any combination of green, yellow, and red peppers works well; I use all three for color. You can also use low-sodium chicken broth and Smart Balance® spread."

Serving: 6 | Prep: 20 m | Cook: 35 m | Ready in: 55 m

Ingredients

- cooking spray
- 1 green bell pepper - halved, seeded, and stem removed
- 1 red bell pepper - halved, seeded, and stem removed
- 1 yellow bell pepper - halved, seeded, and stem removed
- 1 tablespoon butter
- 2 tablespoons olive oil
- 3 green onions, sliced
- 4 cloves garlic, minced
- 2 skinless, boneless chicken breast halves, cut into 1/2-inch cubes
- 1 teaspoon ground black pepper
- 1 teaspoon ground cumin
- 1 cup orzo
- 1 (16 ounce) can chicken broth
- 3 tablespoons Parmesan cheese
- 1 teaspoon olive oil
- 1 teaspoon butter
- 2 portobello mushrooms, thinly sliced
- 1 green onion, thinly sliced
- salt and ground black pepper to taste

Direction

- Preheat the oven to 375 degrees F (190 degrees C).
- Spray inside of green, red, and yellow bell pepper halves with cooking spray; place on a baking sheet.
- Bake peppers in the preheated oven until slightly tender, about 10 minutes.
- Heat 1 tablespoon butter and 2 tablespoons oil in a skillet over medium heat; cook and stir 3 green onions and garlic until fragrant, 2 to 3 minutes. Add chicken, black pepper, and cumin; cook until chicken is no longer pink in the center and juices run clear, 4 to 5 minutes. Add orzo and chicken broth; simmer until orzo is cooked through but firm to the bite and broth is absorbed, about 11 minutes. Spoon chicken-orzo mixture into the bell peppers; sprinkle with Parmesan cheese.
- Bake in the preheated oven until cheese is melted, about 7 minutes.
- Heat 1 teaspoon oil and 1 teaspoon butter in skillet; Cook and stir portobello mushrooms and remaining green onion until tender, about 5 minutes. Season with salt and black pepper. Spoon about 2 tablespoons mushroom mixture onto each stuffed bell pepper.

Nutrition Information

- Calories: 294 calories
- Total Fat: 10.8 g
- Cholesterol: 33 mg
- Sodium: 476 mg
- Total Carbohydrate: 33.2 g
- Protein: 16 g

85. Pan Fried Fingerling Potatoes with Wild Mushroom Sauce

"Fingerling potatoes and wild mushrooms are finished in a creamy mustard and creme fraiche sauce."

Serving: 6 | Prep: 20 m | Cook: 50 m | Ready in: 1 h 10 m

Ingredients

- 2 tablespoons butter
- 1 1/2 pounds fingerling potatoes, halved lengthwise
- 2 cups sliced mixed wild mushrooms (small portobella, crimini, shiitake)
- 2 cloves garlic, minced
- 1 large shallot, thinly sliced
- 1 cup chicken broth
- 1/4 cup dried mixed wild mushrooms
- 2 teaspoons Dijon mustard
- 3/4 teaspoon herbes de Provence
- 1/2 cup creme fraiche or heavy cream
- Freshly ground black pepper to taste
- Chopped fresh thyme

Direction

- Melt butter in a large skillet over medium heat. Add potatoes; cook, stirring occasionally, for 30 minutes or until potatoes are tender. (Tenting with foil will speed up cooking.)
- Stir in fresh mushrooms, garlic and shallot; cook for 10 minutes more. Add broth, dried mushrooms, mustard and herbs; cook

over high heat for 5 minutes or until most of the broth has cooked off. Stir in creme fraiche and cook for 5 minutes more. Season with pepper and fresh thyme.

Nutrition Information

- Calories: 240 calories
- Total Fat: 11.6 g
- Cholesterol: 38 mg
- Sodium: 256 mg
- Total Carbohydrate: 30.5 g
- Protein: 5.2 g

86. Pasta Shells with Portobello Mushrooms and Asparagus in Boursin Sauce

"From my friend Tasneem - an easy recipe to prepare, resulting in a downright sophisticated dish. Asparagus and pasta are tossed with a cheesy mushroom sauce."

Serving: 6 | Prep: 15 m | Cook: 25 m | Ready in: 40 m

Ingredients

- 1 tablespoon butter
- 1 tablespoon olive oil
- 1 pound portobello mushrooms, stems removed
- 1/2 teaspoon salt
- 1 1/4 cups low-sodium chicken broth
- 1 (5.2 ounce) package pepper Boursin cheese
- 3/4 pound uncooked pasta shells
- 1 pound fresh asparagus, trimmed

Direction

- In a large skillet over medium heat, melt the butter and heat the olive oil. Cut the mushroom caps in half, and slice 1/4 inch thick. Cook mushrooms in the skillet 8 minutes, or until tender and lightly browned. Season with salt. Stir in the chicken broth and Boursin cheese. Reduce heat and simmer, stirring constantly, until well blended.
- Bring a large pot of lightly salted water to a boil. Add shell pasta and cook for 5 minutes. Place the asparagus into the pot, and

continue cooking 5 minutes, until the pasta is al dente and the asparagus is tender; drain. Toss with the mushroom sauce to serve.

Nutrition Information

- Calories: 400 calories
- Total Fat: 16.6 g
- Cholesterol: 35 mg
- Sodium: 388 mg
- Total Carbohydrate: 51.6 g
- Protein: 14.1 g

87. Pastini Soup

"This is a light soup of 10,000 stars (pastini). This pasta is hard to find, but worth the search. Serve with grated Parmesan cheese on top and some crusty bread, if desired."

Serving: 4 | Prep: 5 m | Cook: 10 m | Ready in: 15 m

Ingredients

- 1 (8 ounce) package dry pastini
- 3 cups veal stock
- 1 grilled portobello mushroom cap, sliced
- 1 tablespoon tomato paste
- 1 tablespoon red wine
- salt and pepper to taste

Direction

- In a large pot, combine pasta, stock, mushroom, tomato paste, wine and salt and pepper to taste. Cook over medium-high heat for 8 to 10 minutes, or until pasta is al dente.

Nutrition Information

- Calories: 229 calories
- Total Fat: 2.3 g
- Cholesterol: 46 mg
- Sodium: 108 mg
- Total Carbohydrate: 39.7 g
- Protein: 11.1 g

88. Penne with Sausage and Portobello Mushrooms

"This is a delicious pasta dish that uses a red wine reduction. Rich, hearty, and surprisingly easy to make. Use your favorite cheese to top."

Serving: 4 | Prep: 20 m | Cook: 1 h | Ready in: 1 h 20 m

Ingredients

- 4 mild Italian sausage links
- 1 (12 ounce) package penne pasta
- 4 tomatoes, diced
- 1/2 pound baby portobello (cremini) mushrooms, chopped
- 1/2 cup chopped red onion
- 3 cloves garlic, chopped
- 1 1/2 cups red wine
- 1 tablespoon crushed dried rosemary
- 1 tablespoon crushed dried oregano
- 1 tablespoon crushed dried thyme
- 1 tablespoon kosher salt
- 1 tablespoon ground black pepper
- 1/2 cup shredded mozzarella cheese

Direction

- Fill a pot with water and bring to a boil; cook the sausages in the boiling water until no longer pink in the center, about 40 minutes. Cut the sausages into bite-sized pieces.
- Fill a large pot with lightly-salted water and bring to a boil. Stir the penne into the water and return to a boil. Cook, stirring

occasionally, until the pasta has cooked through, but is still firm to the bite, about 11 minutes. Drain well.
- Combine the tomatoes, mushrooms, onion, garlic, wine, rosemary, oregano, thyme, salt, and pepper in a large skillet over medium heat; cook and stir until the liquid is reduced to about half its original volume, about 10 minutes. Add the sausage and the drained pasta to the mixture and continue cooking until the liquid is reduced to about one-quarter its original volume, 10 to 15 minutes more. Sprinkle the mozzarella cheese over the dish to serve.

Nutrition Information

- Calories: 679 calories
- Total Fat: 21 g
- Cholesterol: 42 mg
- Sodium: 2254 mg
- Total Carbohydrate: 80.6 g
- Protein: 29.3 g

89. Penne with Yogurt Tahini Sauce

"This simple sauce can be prepared while the pasta is cooking. The vegetable saute is optional."

Serving: 8 | Prep: 20 m | Cook: 20 m | Ready in: 40 m

Ingredients

- 3 tablespoons tahini
- 1/8 cup lemon juice
- 1 cup plain yogurt
- 3/4 cup water
- 3 cloves garlic
- 1/4 cup olive oil
- 1 onion, chopped
- 2 large portobello mushrooms, sliced
- 1/2 red bell pepper, diced
- 1 (16 ounce) package penne pasta
- 1/2 cup chopped parsley
- ground black pepper to taste

Direction

- In a large pot of lightly salted boiling water, cook pasta 10 to 12 minutes, or until al dente.
- While pasta is cooking, stir together tahini and lemon juice. Place in a food processor with yogurt, water, and garlic cloves; process until smooth.

- Heat the oil in a sauté pan over medium heat. Add the onion, and cook until soft. Add the mushrooms, and cook until soft. During the final few minutes of cooking add the bell pepper; the pepper should be still crispish.
- Drain the pasta. Toss with the yogurt-tahini sauce, chopped parsley, and freshly ground black pepper. Serve the vegetable sauté over the noodles.

Nutrition Information

- Calories: 332 calories
- Total Fat: 11.7 g
- Cholesterol: 2 mg
- Sodium: 36 mg
- Total Carbohydrate: 48.2 g
- Protein: 11.1 g

90. Peppered Shrimp Alfredo

"Yummy shrimp in an Alfredo sauce, with portobello mushrooms and red peppers."

Serving: 6 | Prep: 30 m | Cook: 20 m | Ready in: 50 m

Ingredients

- 12 ounces penne pasta
- 1/4 cup butter
- 2 tablespoons extra-virgin olive oil
- 1 onion, diced
- 2 cloves garlic, minced
- 1 red bell pepper, diced
- 1/2 pound portobello mushrooms, diced
- 1 pound medium shrimp, peeled and deveined
- 1 (15 ounce) jar Alfredo sauce
- 1/2 cup grated Romano cheese
- 1/2 cup cream
- 1 teaspoon cayenne pepper, or more to taste
- Salt and pepper to taste
- 1/4 cup chopped parsley

Direction

- Bring a large pot of lightly salted water to a boil. Add pasta and cook for 8 to 10 minutes or until al dente; drain.
- Meanwhile, melt butter together with the olive oil in a saucepan over medium heat. Stir in onion, and cook until softened and translucent, about 2 minutes. Stir in garlic, red pepper, and

mushroom; cook over medium-high heat until soft, about 2 minutes more.
- Stir in the shrimp, and cook until firm and pink, then pour in Alfredo sauce, Romano cheese, and cream; bring to a simmer stirring constantly until thickened, about 5 minutes. Season with cayenne, salt, and pepper to taste. Stir drained pasta into the sauce, and serve sprinkled with chopped parsley.

Nutrition Information

- Calories: 707 calories
- Total Fat: 45 g
- Cholesterol: 201 mg
- Sodium: 1034 mg
- Total Carbohydrate: 50.6 g
- Protein: 28.4 g

91. Personal Portobello Pizza

"A delicious recipe that substitutes a portobello mushroom for a pizza crust. Try using pesto sauce instead of spaghetti sauce, and experiment with your favorite pizza toppings."

Serving: 1 | Prep: 15 m | Cook: 25 m | Ready in: 40 m

Ingredients

- 1 large portobello mushroom, stem removed
- 1 tablespoon spaghetti sauce
- 1/2 cup mozzarella cheese
- 1/2 tablespoon sliced black olives
- 4 slices pepperoni sausage
- 1 clove garlic, chopped

Direction

- Preheat the oven to 375 degrees F (190 degrees C).
- Place the mushroom on a baking sheet, and bake for 5 minutes in the preheated oven. Remove from the oven, and spread spaghetti sauce in the cup of the cap. Top with cheese, olives, pepperoni and garlic.
- Bake for an additional 20 minutes, or until cheese is melted and golden.

Nutrition Information

- Calories: 235 calories
- Total Fat: 13.6 g
- Cholesterol: 45 mg

- Sodium: 590 mg
- Total Carbohydrate: 10.6 g
- Protein: 18.8 g

92. PestoStuffed Grilled Portobellos

"Pesto-stuffed grilled portobellos make for the perfect summer outdoor meal. It stands alone as vegetarian fare if you serve it with fresh fruit (such as watermelon chunks and blueberries); I love it with cedar-plank grilled salmon as well. You will think you've died and gone to heaven."

Serving: 3 | Prep: 10 m | Cook: 20 m | Ready in: 40 m

Ingredients

- 6 portobello mushrooms
- 1 tablespoon olive oil
- 1 small shallot, minced
- 1 clove garlic, minced
- 1 splash Chardonnay wine, or as desired
- 3 tablespoons pesto
- 2 tablespoons pine nuts
- 1/2 cup shredded Italian 3-cheese blend

Direction

- Remove stems from mushrooms and finely chop stems.
- Heat olive oil in a skillet over medium heat; cook and stir chopped mushroom stems, shallot, and garlic until softened, about 5 minutes. Pour wine into the skillet; cook and stir mixture using a wooden spoon until liquid is evaporated, 1 to 2 minutes. Cool mixture to room temperature, about 10 minutes.
- Preheat an outdoor grill for medium heat and lightly oil the grate.

- Brush the olive oil mixture over the top each mushroom and place, top-side up, on a grilling pan. Mix pesto and pine nuts with the mushroom stem mixture together in a bowl; spoon into each mushroom. Sprinkle Italian cheese blend over the filling.
- Grill mushrooms on the preheated grill until edges are blackened and stuffing is bubbling, about 10 minutes.

Nutrition Information

- Calories: 282 calories
- Total Fat: 20.2 g
- Cholesterol: 20 mg
- Sodium: 297 mg
- Total Carbohydrate: 15.4 g
- Protein: 14.5 g

93. PizzaStyle Portabello Mushrooms

"These are to die for if you are a vegetarian, or just love great spicy pizza without all the calories. I stumbled across these prepackaged and decided to make them part of my recipe box because they are so yummy and easy to prepare for family or guests. Portabello mushroom topped with cheese, tomato, spices, black olives and balsamic vinaigrette."

Serving: 2 | Prep: 15 m | Cook: 30 m | Ready in: 45 m

Ingredients

- 2 large portobello mushroom caps
- 1/2 cup diced tomatoes
- 2 tablespoons balsamic vinegar
- 1 tablespoon olive oil
- 1 tablespoon chopped fresh basil
- 2 cloves garlic, chopped
- 1 pinch dried parsley, or to taste
- 1 pinch red pepper flakes, or to taste
- 4 ounces shredded pepperjack cheese
- 4 ounces shredded mozzarella cheese
- 2 tablespoons sliced black olives, or to taste (optional)
- 1 tablespoon Italian-style seasoned bread crumbs, or to taste

Direction

- Preheat oven to 350 degrees F (175 degrees C). Place mushrooms in a baking dish.
- Cook and stir tomatoes, balsamic vinegar, olive oil, basil, garlic, parsley, and red pepper flakes in a large skillet over medium

heat until heated through, 5 to 10 minutes.
- Top each mushroom with 1/2 of the tomato mixture. Sprinkle pepperjack cheese and mozzarella cheese on top of tomato mixture; top with black olives and bread crumbs.
- Bake in the preheated oven until golden brown and crispy, about 25 minutes.

Nutrition Information

- Calories: 477 calories
- Total Fat: 35.4 g
- Cholesterol: 97 mg
- Sodium: 845 mg
- Total Carbohydrate: 12.4 g
- Protein: 27.4 g

94. Portabella Basil Sub

"Portabella mushrooms are cooked in butter with spinach, yellow pepper, garlic, basil and shallots, and served on a roll."

Serving: 1 | Prep: 23 m | Cook: 7 m | Ready in: 30 m

Ingredients

- 1 tablespoon butter
- 1/4 cup chopped red shallots
- 2 tablespoons chopped fresh basil leaves
- 1 tablespoon minced fresh garlic
- 1 teaspoon hot paprika
- 1 teaspoon salt
- 1 teaspoon fresh ground black pepper
- 1 cup fresh spinach leaves
- 1/4 cup diced portabella mushroom caps
- 1/4 cup diced yellow bell pepper
- 1 tablespoon sweet Jamaican pepper sauce (such as Pickapeppa Sauce ®)
- 1 tablespoon balsamic vinegar
- 1 hoagie roll, split lengthwise

Direction

- Melt the butter in a skillet with a lid over medium heat, and cook and stir the red shallots, basil, and garlic until fragrant, about 1 minute. Stir in the hot paprika, salt, and pepper. Add the spinach, portabella mushrooms, and yellow bell pepper, stir a few times, cover with lid, and reduce the heat to medium-low.

Cook the mixture until the spinach and mushrooms give up their liquid and the peppers are softened, about 4 minutes.
- Uncover the skillet, and pour in the pepper sauce and balsamic vinegar. Increase the heat to medium, and let the mixture cook down and thicken slightly, about 2 minutes.
- Spoon the hot mushroom mixture onto the split hoagie roll, and serve.

Nutrition Information

- Calories: 568 calories
- Total Fat: 18.9 g
- Cholesterol: 31 mg
- Sodium: 3200 mg
- Total Carbohydrate: 85.8 g
- Protein: 15.4 g

95. Portabello Mushroom and Pepper Risotto

"I haven't seen any recipes with bell peppers in it, so I decided to try this on my own. Had a 6-person dinner party that I served with some bone-in pork chops. I first thought I made too much, but all of my guests were upset that there wasn't more. Hope you like it."

Serving: 6 | Prep: 15 m | Cook: 40 m | Ready in: 1 h

Ingredients

- 3 tablespoons olive oil
- 1 sweet onion (such as Vidalia®), diced
- 1 green bell pepper, diced
- 4 large portobello mushroom caps, cut into 1/2-inch slices
- kosher salt and ground black pepper to taste
- 2 cups Arborio rice
- 3/4 cup dry white wine
- 6 cups chicken stock, or more if needed
- 1/2 cup heavy cream
- 1/2 cup grated Parmesan cheese

Direction

- Heat olive oil in a large skillet over medium-low heat. Cook onion in hot oil until softened, about 3 minutes. Add bell pepper and portobello mushrooms to the skillet, season with kosher salt and pepper, and continue cooking another 10 minutes.
- Stir Arborio rice into the mushroom mixture. Pour white wine into the skillet; cook and stir until the wine is warmed. Add chicken stock 1 1/2 cups at a time, stirring continually to allow

each addition to absorb into the rice before adding the next, until all stock is integrated, 20 to 30 minutes. Stir heavy cream into the rice mixture; cook about 1 minute. Remove the skillet from heat and stir Parmesan cheese into the risotto. Let sit 5 to 10 minutes before serving.

Nutrition Information

- Calories: 477 calories
- Total Fat: 16.7 g
- Cholesterol: 34 mg
- Sodium: 865 mg
- Total Carbohydrate: 66.7 g
- Protein: 9.1 g

96. Portobello Artichoke Soup

"This soup has a great mix of fresh delicate flavors. It's sure to be one of your favorites too."

Serving: 4 | Prep: 25 m | Cook: 37 m | Ready in: 1 h 2 m

Ingredients

- 1/2 cup butter, divided
- 2 carrots, peeled and diced
- 2 stalks celery, sliced
- 1/2 cup chopped green onions
- 2 portobello mushrooms, chopped
- 4 cups chicken broth
- 2 (14 ounce) cans artichoke hearts, drained and sliced
- 3/4 teaspoon dried thyme
- 3/4 teaspoon dried oregano
- 1/4 teaspoon ground cayenne pepper
- 2 bay leaves
- 1/4 cup all-purpose flour
- 1/2 cup milk
- 1 cup heavy whipping cream

Direction

- Melt 1/4 cup butter in a large pot over medium heat. Add carrots, celery, and green onions; cook and stir until starting to brown, about 10 minutes. Stir in portobello mushrooms; cook until softened, 3 to 4 minutes.
- Pour chicken broth into the pot. Add artichoke hearts, thyme, oregano, cayenne pepper, and bay leaves. Simmer soup until

flavors combine, 15 to 20 minutes.
- Melt remaining 1/4 cup butter in a small skillet over low heat. Add flour; cook and stir until a paste forms, about 1 minute. Pour in milk. Bring to a simmer and cook, stirring constantly, until thickened, about 5 minutes.
- Pour milk mixture into the soup. Stir in heavy cream slowly. Simmer until soup is slightly thickened and heated through, 3 to 5 minutes. Discard bay leaves before serving.

Nutrition Information

- Calories: 560 calories
- Total Fat: 46.5 g
- Cholesterol: 150 mg
- Sodium: 1931 mg
- Total Carbohydrate: 29.1 g
- Protein: 9.7 g

97. Portobello Bellybuttons

"Mushrooms and tortellini are mixed with a butter, garlic, and wine sauce. Tortellini looks like bellybuttons. This is a very quick and versatile meal."

Serving: 4 | Prep: 15 m | Cook: 15 m | Ready in: 30 m

Ingredients

- 1 (16 ounce) package cheese tortellini
- 3 tablespoons butter
- 1 clove garlic, minced
- 2 portobello mushrooms, chopped
- 1/2 pound button mushrooms, sliced
- 1/4 cup white wine
- 1/2 tablespoon dried basil
- salt and pepper to taste
- 1/2 cup grated Parmesan cheese

Direction

- Bring a large pot of lightly salted water to a boil. Add pasta and cook until al dente; drain.
- While water is boiling, melt the butter in a skillet and cook the garlic until fragrant. Stir in portobello mushrooms, button mushrooms, white wine, and basil. Season with salt and pepper to taste. Continue to cook until mushrooms are tender. Pour mushroom mixture into drained pasta and stir. Top with grated Parmesan cheese and serve.

Nutrition Information

- Calories: 512 calories
- Total Fat: 21.6 g
- Cholesterol: 81 mg
- Sodium: 778 mg
- Total Carbohydrate: 57.8 g
- Protein: 22.6 g

98. Portobello Bruschetta with Three Cheeses

"I used a portobello mushroom cap instead of the traditional ciabatta bread. I added cheese to enhance the main-course appeal."

Serving: 2 | Prep: 10 m | Cook: 8 m | Ready in: 18 m

Ingredients

- 2 Roma (plum) tomatoes, diced
- 1/2 cup crumbled feta cheese
- 2 cups arugula, chopped
- 4 cloves garlic, minced
- 2 large portobello mushroom caps
- 2 tablespoons olive oil
- 2 tablespoons grated Parmesan cheese
- 4 slices fontina cheese
- salt and pepper to taste

Direction

- Preheat an oven to 425 degrees F (220 degrees C). Lightly grease a large baking sheet. Combine tomatoes, feta, arugula, and garlic in a small bowl.
- Arrange mushroom caps, stem side up, on the prepared baking sheet. Drizzle each with 1 tablespoon olive oil and season with salt and pepper. Roast in preheated oven until mushrooms begin to soften, 5 to 7 minutes. Remove from oven.
- Sprinkle caps with Parmesan cheese; divide tomato mixture evenly between each mushroom cap. Season with salt and

pepper; drizzle with remaining 2 tablespoons olive oil. Top each mushroom with 2 slices of fontina cheese.
- Return to oven until cheese is melted, but tomato mixture is still cool in the center, about 3 minutes.

Nutrition Information

- Calories: 486 calories
- Total Fat: 40.9 g
- Cholesterol: 104 mg
- Sodium: 958 mg
- Total Carbohydrate: 7.8 g
- Protein: 23.2 g

99. Portobello Burgers with Goat Cheese

"Delicious broiled portobello mushrooms layered with goat cheese, roasted beets, and a pseudo aioli sauce. Yum!"

Serving: 4 | Cook: 50 m | Ready in: 50 m

Ingredients

- 2 medium beets
- 1/4 cup olive oil
- 2 tablespoons balsamic vinegar
- 1 teaspoon dried rosemary
- 2 cloves garlic, minced and divided
- 4 portobello mushroom caps
- 1/2 cup goat cheese
- 4 sandwich buns, split and toasted
- 1 1/2 cups baby spinach leaves
- 3 tablespoons mayonnaise
- 2 cloves garlic, minced
- 2 limes, juiced

Direction

- Preheat an oven to 400 degrees F (200 degrees C).
- Cut the tops off the beets and place them in a baking dish with enough water to cover the bottom of the dish.
- Roast the beets in the preheated oven until they are easily pierced with a knife, 40 to 50 minutes. Refrigerate until cool. Slice and set aside.

- Preheat the oven's broiler and set the oven rack to the second level from the heat source.
- Whisk the olive oil, balsamic vinegar, rosemary, and 2 cloves minced garlic together in a bowl. Spread about half of this mixture over the ribbed side of the portobello mushroom caps; arrange the mushrooms on a baking sheet with the ribbed sides facing upwards.
- Broil the mushrooms until tender, making sure to not burn the garlic, 5 to 7 minutes. Flip the mushrooms and brush the remaining olive oil mixture over the tops of the caps. Return to the oven and broil until tender, about 5 minutes more.
- Spread equal amounts of the goat cheese on one half of each of the sandwich rolls. Top each with a portion of the sliced beets and the spinach. Whisk the mayonnaise, garlic, and lime juice together in a bowl; spread evenly over the remaining sandwich roll halves and top with one mushroom cap each. Bring the two halves together to form the sandwiches to serve.

Nutrition Information

- Calories: 489 calories
- Total Fat: 32.8 g
- Cholesterol: 26 mg
- Sodium: 497 mg
- Total Carbohydrate: 38.5 g
- Protein: 14.1 g

100. Portobello Chicken

"A quick and easy but delicious dinner entree perfect for surprise guests. I serve with wild rice and use the leftover sauce in the rice. Do not use too much seasoning on the chicken, otherwise the dish turns out too salty."

Serving: 4 | Prep: 5 m | Cook: 40 m | Ready in: 45 m

Ingredients

- 1 tablespoon olive oil
- 3 portobello mushrooms, cut into strips
- 1 (750 milliliter) bottle Merlot wine
- 4 cooked chicken breast halves
- 4 slices provolone cheese

Direction

- Preheat oven to 350 degrees F (175 degrees C).
- Heat olive oil in a skillet over medium heat. Cook and stir mushrooms in hot oil until warmed, 2 to 3 minutes. Pour wine over the mushrooms, bring to a simmer, and cook until the wine becomes thick and the mushrooms tender, about 35 minutes.
- Arrange chicken on a serving platter; top each with a slice of provolone cheese. Pour mushroom and merlot sauce over the chicken.

Nutrition Information

- Calories: 427 calories
- Total Fat: 15.8 g
- Cholesterol: 67 mg

- Sodium: 300 mg
- Total Carbohydrate: 9.7 g
- Protein: 26.9 g

101. Portobello Lemon Chicken

"From the maker of 'Greasy Chicken' comes my signature dish, the most requested and favored chicken, ever! The mushrooms and onions taste great after cooking in the lemon juice, and it is especially good when marinated ahead of time."

Serving: 4 | Prep: 15 m | Cook: 40 m | Ready in: 55 m

Ingredients

- 1 large yellow onion, chopped
- 2 portobello mushroom caps, chopped
- 2 pounds bone-in chicken pieces
- garlic salt to taste
- ground black pepper to taste
- 2 large lemons, juiced

Direction

- Preheat oven to 400 degrees F (200 degrees C).
- Spread the chopped onion and mushrooms evenly in the bottom of a 9x13 inch baking dish. Arrange chicken pieces over the vegetables, skin side up. Squeeze lemon juice over the chicken pieces, and season with garlic salt and pepper.
- Bake chicken uncovered for 20 minutes in the preheated oven. Carefully turn the pieces over, and continue cooking 15 minutes more.
- Set oven to broil. Cook chicken for 5 minutes, or until chicken skin is crisp.

Nutrition Information

- Calories: 328 calories
- Total Fat: 17.5 g
- Cholesterol: 97 mg
- Sodium: 250 mg
- Total Carbohydrate: 12.6 g
- Protein: 33.2 g

102. Portobello Mushroom Appetizer

"A great appetizer for entertaining company. Very easy to make, quick and simple."

Serving: 6 | Prep: 15 m | Cook: 15 m | Ready in: 30 m

Ingredients

- 2 cloves garlic, minced
- 1/4 cup olive oil
- 6 portobello mushrooms
- 1 1/2 cups diced tomato
- 4 ounces blue cheese, crumbled

Direction

- Preheat oven to 375 degrees F (190 degrees C).
- In a small bowl stir together the minced garlic and olive oil. Clean portobello mushrooms by brushing them with a paper towel. Remove the stem and discard. Brush the mushroom caps with the garlic and olive oil mixture. Place them on a baking sheet with gills facing upward Sprinkle 1/4 cup of diced tomatoes on each mushroom cap.
- Bake for 13 minutes in the preheated oven. Remove from the oven and spread blue cheese on top of the tomatoes. Return the mushrooms to the oven and bake until the cheese is melted and bubbly. Allow the mushrooms to cool for a few minutes before serving.

Nutrition Information

- Calories: 185 calories
- Total Fat: 14.8 g
- Cholesterol: 14 mg
- Sodium: 273 mg
- Total Carbohydrate: 8.2 g
- Protein: 7.3 g

103. Portobello Mushroom Bolognese Sauce

"This is a vegetarian option I created for Bolognese sauce - and it could fool the unsuspecting! Serve over pasta with Parmesan cheese. Enjoy!"

Serving: 4 | Prep: 15 m | Cook: 3 h 22 m | Ready in: 3 h 37 m

Ingredients

- 1 onion, quartered
- 1 large stalk celery, halved
- 1 carrot, quartered
- 4 large portobello mushrooms, stemmed
- 1 tablespoon vegetable oil, or to taste
- salt to taste
- 1/2 cup white wine
- 1/4 cup milk
- 1/4 teaspoon ground nutmeg
- 2 (15 ounce) cans whole tomatoes, or more to taste
- 1/2 cup water (optional)

Direction

- Pulse onion in a food processor until diced but not mushy. Transfer to a bowl. Repeat with celery and carrot. Pulse portobello mushrooms to the consistency of ground beef.
- Coat the bottom of a large pot with oil; heat over low heat. Cook and stir onion in the oil until soft but not browned, about 5 minutes. Stir in celery and carrot; cook until slightly softened,

about 5 minutes. Add portobello mushrooms; cook about 1 minute. Season with salt.
- Pour wine into the pot. Increase heat to medium-high; stir with a flat wooden spoon until bottom of the pot looks almost dry, 3 to 5 minutes. Add milk and nutmeg. Reduce heat to medium; cook and stir until bottom of the pot is almost dry, 3 to 5 minutes.
- Pour tomato juice from the cans into the pot. Pulse tomatoes in the food processor until coarsely chopped; stir into the pot. Bring to a boil; reduce heat to low and simmer until flavors combine, 3 to 4 hours. Thin sauce with water if it appears too thick.

Nutrition Information

- Calories: 128 calories
- Total Fat: 4.1 g
- Cholesterol: 1 mg
- Sodium: 368 mg
- Total Carbohydrate: 16.5 g
- Protein: 3 g

104. Portobello Mushroom Burger With Bruschetta Topping

"I'm always looking to do something new since my wife and daughter turned vegetarian. She brought home some fresh picked portobellos from work so I made them into burgers and had some tomatoes to use up, which I made into bruschetta topping, and thus this burger was born."

Serving: 2 | Prep: 20 m | Cook: 30 m | Ready in: 1 h 50 m

Ingredients

- 8 roma (plum) tomatoes, diced
- 1/3 cup chopped fresh basil
- 1/4 cup shredded Parmesan cheese
- 1 tablespoon balsamic vinegar
- 2 cloves garlic, minced
- 1 teaspoon olive oil
- 1/2 teaspoon kosher salt
- 1/2 teaspoon ground black pepper
- 2 large portobello mushroom caps, stems removed
- 2 tablespoons shredded horseradish Cheddar cheese, or to taste (optional)
- 2 kaiser rolls, split

Direction

- Mix roma tomatoes, basil, Parmesan cheese, balsamic vinegar, garlic, olive oil, kosher salt, and black pepper in a bowl and refrigerate to blend flavors, 1 to 2 hours.
- Preheat grill for medium heat and lightly oil the grate.

- Grill portobello mushrooms with gill sides up on an upper rack of the grill until juicy and hot, about 15 minutes. Spoon tomato mixture into mushroom caps to cover entire cap. Continue grilling until topping is heated through, another 15 to 20 minutes. Top with horseradish Cheddar cheese if desired; grill until cheese has melted, 1 to 2 more minutes. Serve on kaiser rolls.

Nutrition Information

- Calories: 269 calories
- Total Fat: 10.1 g
- Cholesterol: 16 mg
- Sodium: 939 mg
- Total Carbohydrate: 34.4 g
- Protein: 12.2 g

105. Portobello Mushroom Burgers

"The steak of veggie burgers. Serve on a bun with lettuce, tomato, and aioli sauce. Oh yeah!"

Serving: 4 | Prep: 15 m | Cook: 20 m | Ready in: 35 m

Ingredients

- 4 portobello mushroom caps
- 1/4 cup balsamic vinegar
- 2 tablespoons olive oil
- 1 teaspoon dried basil
- 1 teaspoon dried oregano
- 1 tablespoon minced garlic
- salt and pepper to taste
- 4 (1 ounce) slices provolone cheese

Direction

- Place the mushroom caps, smooth side up, in a shallow dish. In a small bowl, whisk together vinegar, oil, basil, oregano, garlic, salt, and pepper. Pour over the mushrooms. Let stand at room temperature for 15 minutes or so, turning twice.
- Preheat grill for medium-high heat.
- Brush grate with oil. Place mushrooms on the grill, reserving marinade for basting. Grill for 5 to 8 minutes on each side, or until tender. Brush with marinade frequently. Top with cheese during the last 2 minutes of grilling.

Nutrition Information

- Calories: 203 calories
- Total Fat: 14.6 g
- Cholesterol: 20 mg
- Sodium: 259 mg
- Total Carbohydrate: 9.8 g
- Protein: 10.3 g

106. Portobello Mushroom Caps and Veggies

"Vegetarian steak! Delicious and fills ya up. Wonderful for company, too! Serve with rice and soy sauce."

Serving: 4 | Prep: 15 m | Cook: 15 m | Ready in: 30 m

Ingredients

- 1 tablespoon olive oil
- 1 tablespoon garlic, peeled and minced
- 1 onion, cut into strips
- 1 green bell pepper, cut into strips
- 1/4 teaspoon salt
- 4 large portobello mushroom caps

Direction

- Heat olive oil in a medium skillet over medium heat. Stir in the garlic, onion, and green bell pepper. Season with salt. Cook about 5 minutes, until vegetables are tender.
- Reduce skillet heat to low. Place mushroom caps in the skillet, cover, and cook about 5 minutes per side, until tender.

Nutrition Information

- Calories: 79 calories
- Total Fat: 3.7 g
- Cholesterol: 0 mg
- Sodium: 154 mg

- Total Carbohydrate: 10.3 g
- Protein: 3.5 g

107. Portobello Mushroom Chili

"This is a very hearty and tasty chili."

Serving: 6 | Prep: 15 m | Cook: 55 m | Ready in: 1 h 10 m

Ingredients

- 2 tablespoons extra virgin olive oil
- 2 medium onions, diced
- 2 cloves garlic, chopped
- 1 tablespoon chili powder
- 1/4 teaspoon ground cayenne pepper
- 1 1/2 pounds portobello mushrooms, cut into 1/2 inch pieces
- 1 (28 ounce) can Italian-style diced tomatoes
- 1 (19 ounce) can red kidney beans
- salt to taste
- 1/2 teaspoon ground black pepper

Direction

- Heat the oil in a large pot over medium heat, and cook the onions until tender. Stir in the garlic, chili powder, and cayenne pepper. Mix the mushrooms into the skillet, and continue cooking, stirring frequently, 10 minutes, or until tender.
- Pour the tomatoes and beans into the skillet. Season with salt and pepper. Reduce heat to low, cover, and simmer 40 minutes.

Nutrition Information

- Calories: 193 calories
- Total Fat: 5.4 g
- Cholesterol: 0 mg
- Sodium: 518 mg
- Total Carbohydrate: 28.4 g
- Protein: 9.4 g

108. Portobello Mushroom Fresh Peppers and Goat Cheese Pizza

"Tons of flavorful ingredients make this pizza unique and delicious. The balsamic vinegar caramelizes and makes a sort of sauce."

Serving: 8 | Prep: 10 m | Cook: 20 m | Ready in: 30 m

Ingredients

- 1 (10 ounce) can refrigerated pizza crust dough
- 1 tablespoon olive oil
- 2 cloves garlic, minced
- 1 red bell pepper, sliced
- 1 yellow bell pepper, sliced
- 2 portobello mushrooms, thinly sliced
- 1 (6.5 ounce) jar marinated artichoke hearts, drained and chopped
- 4 ounces goat cheese, crumbled
- 3 tablespoons balsamic vinegar

Direction

- Preheat the oven to 350 degrees F (175 degrees C). Grease a baking sheet, or round pizza pan.
- Spread pizza dough out evenly on the prepared pan. Drizzle with olive oil. Sprinkle the garlic over the crust. Arrange red and yellow bell peppers, mushrooms and artichoke hearts on top, then dot with pieces of goat cheese. Drizzle balsamic vinegar over the top.

- Bake for 15 to 20 minutes in the preheated oven, until the edges are golden brown.

Nutrition Information

- Calories: 200 calories
- Total Fat: 8.5 g
- Cholesterol: 11 mg
- Sodium: 396 mg
- Total Carbohydrate: 23.8 g
- Protein: 8 g

109. Portobello Mushroom Lentil Soup

"This is a very easy and flavorful lentil soup that is perfect for a cold winter day!"

Serving: 8 | Prep: 20 m | Cook: 30 m | Ready in: 50 m

Ingredients

- 2 cups chopped portobello mushrooms
- 1 green bell pepper, chopped
- 1 small red onion, chopped
- 1 tablespoon olive oil
- 4 cloves garlic, chopped
- 1 (6 ounce) can tomato paste
- 6 cups chicken broth
- 4 teaspoons dried basil, or to taste
- 1 1/2 cups dried brown lentils, rinsed and drained
- salt and pepper to taste
- 1/4 cup cooking sherry
- grated Parmesan cheese

Direction

- Heat oil in a large pot over medium heat. Add mushrooms, green pepper, onion and garlic, and sauté until tender, about 5 minutes. Pour in the chicken broth, and stir in the tomato paste. Bring to a boil, and add the lentils. Reduce heat to low, cover, and simmer for about 15 minutes. Season with basil, salt and pepper. Cover and simmer for another 15 minutes.

- Ladle into bowls, and top each bowl with 1 tablespoon of sherry and sprinkle with Parmesan cheese to taste.

Nutrition Information

- Calories: 198 calories
- Total Fat: 3.2 g
- Cholesterol: 3 mg
- Sodium: 302 mg
- Total Carbohydrate: 30.7 g
- Protein: 12.5 g

110. Portobello Mushroom Pasta

"A quick and easy pasta dish that utilizes lots of vegetables. Very healthy, too!"

Serving: 4

Ingredients

- 1 (16 ounce) package farfalle pasta
- 2 tablespoons olive oil
- 3 cloves garlic, minced
- 1/2 pound chopped portabello mushrooms
- 1 red bell pepper, diced
- 1 zucchini, cut into 1/2-inch slices
- 1/4 cup red wine vinegar
- 2 tablespoons grated Parmesan cheese

Direction

- In a large pot with boiling salted water cook farfalle pasta until al dente. Drain.
- Meanwhile, in a large non-stick skillet over medium heat cook the garlic, mushrooms, red bell pepper, and zucchini until soft, about 10 minutes. Stir frequently. Stir in red wine vinegar.
- Toss cooked pasta with mushroom mixture. Top with grated Parmesan cheese. Serve warm.

Nutrition Information

- Calories: 507 calories
- Total Fat: 10.3 g

- Cholesterol: 2 mg
- Sodium: 56 mg
- Total Carbohydrate: 88.8 g
- Protein: 18.3 g

111. Portobello Mushroom Pasta with Basil

"Balsamic vinegar gives a piquant edge to sauteed garlic and portobello mushrooms. Toss the mixture with bow-tie pasta and serve with shaved Pecorino Romano cheese and fresh chopped basil."

Serving: 4 | Prep: 10 m | Cook: 25 m | Ready in: 35 m

Ingredients

- 1 (16 ounce) package farfalle (bow-tie) pasta
- 2 tablespoons olive oil
- 1 pound portobello mushrooms, chopped
- 3 cloves garlic, minced
- 1/4 cup balsamic vinegar
- 1 teaspoon ground black pepper
- 1/2 cup shaved Pecorino Romano cheese
- 1/2 cup chopped fresh basil

Direction

- Bring a large pot of lightly salted water to a boil. Cook the bow-tie pasta at a boil, stirring occasionally, until cooked through yet firm to the bite, about 12 minutes; drain and return pasta to the pot.
- While the pasta boils, heat olive oil in a large non-stick skillet over medium heat; cook and stir mushrooms and garlic in hot oil until the mushrooms are softened, about 10 minutes. Drizzle balsamic vinegar into the mushroom mixture while stirring.
- Stir mushroom mixture into the pasta in the pot; season with pepper and stir. Top with Pecorino Romano cheese and basil.

Nutrition Information

- Calories: 564 calories
- Total Fat: 13.7 g
- Cholesterol: 15 mg
- Sodium: 196 mg
- Total Carbohydrate: 91.4 g
- Protein: 22.9 g

112. Portobello Mushroom Pizzas

"This recipe is light and quick and requires only a few basic ingredients. If you love pizza like we do, but are looking for a healthier alternative, give this recipe a try. You can experiment with different ingredients and add your own toppings."

Serving: 4 | Prep: 25 m | Cook: 23 m | Ready in: 48 m

Ingredients

- olive oil cooking spray
- 2 tablespoons olive oil
- 1 onion, chopped
- 4 tomatoes, diced
- 1 leek, chopped
- 4 cloves garlic, chopped
- 1 pinch salt
- 1 tablespoon fresh lemon juice
- 5 leaves fresh basil, chopped
- 4 large portobello mushroom caps
- 1/4 cup grated Parmigiano-Reggiano cheese
- 1 tablespoon chopped fresh parsley

Direction

- Preheat oven to 400 degrees F (200 degrees C). Grease a baking sheet with cooking spray.
- Heat olive oil in a saucepan over medium heat. Cook and stir onion in hot oil until slightly browned, about 5 minutes. Add tomatoes, leek, garlic, and salt; sauté until tomatoes are soft, about 5 minutes more. Sprinkle lemon juice over the vegetable mixture. Stir in basil; heat until wilted, about 1 minute.

- Arrange portobello mushroom caps onto the prepared baking sheet. Fill mushroom caps with onion mixture. Sprinkle Parmigiano-Reggiano cheese on top.
- Bake in the preheated oven until mushrooms are heated through and the Parmigiano-Reggiano cheese has melted, about 12 minutes. Sprinkle with parsley.

Nutrition Information

- Calories: 128 calories
- Total Fat: 8.4 g
- Cholesterol: 4 mg
- Sodium: 124 mg
- Total Carbohydrate: 10.8 g
- Protein: 3.3 g

113. Portobello Mushroom Ravioli with Prawns

"This is a sinfully rich pasta with Portobello mushrooms, prawns and capers in a white wine, butter and garlic sauce."

Serving: 4 | Prep: 25 m | Cook: 15 m | Ready in: 40 m

Ingredients

- 20 large prawns, peeled and deveined
- 12 ounces prepared fresh cheese ravioli
- 7 large portobello mushrooms, sliced
- 3 cloves garlic, minced
- 3 tablespoons capers
- 3/8 cup butter
- 5 fluid ounces white wine
- 2 tablespoons olive oil
- freshly ground black pepper
- 2 tablespoons grated Parmesan cheese
- 1/2 lemon, juiced

Direction

- Have a stock pot of water near boiling before starting the sauce for this recipe! If you're fast at making the sauce, throw in ravioli when you begin to make the sauce. If not, cook ravioli according to package directions.
- In a large saucepan, melt 1/4 cup of butter or margarine over a medium heat. Sauté garlic for 1 to 2 minutes. Stir in olive oil

and capers. Add 4 ounces of white wine and prawns, and bring to a boil.
- Reduce heat and simmer for 2 to 3 minutes, letting wine reduce. Stir in sliced mushrooms, and additional butter and wine so that the sauce is thick, but still liquid after 2 to 3 minutes. Stir in lemon juice, and add fresh pepper to taste.
- To serve, place raviolis on 4 plates, then place 5 to 6 prawns on each plate. Evenly distribute the remaining sauce between the four plates, and garnish with lots of freshly grated parmesan cheese!

Nutrition Information

- Calories: 576 calories
- Total Fat: 32.3 g
- Cholesterol: 82 mg
- Sodium: 509 mg
- Total Carbohydrate: 43.5 g
- Protein: 25.9 g

114. Portobello Mushroom Sauce

"A decadent sauce for steak, also great for dipping French bread."

Serving: 8 | Prep: 5 m | Cook: 20 m | Ready in: 25 m

Ingredients

- 1/4 cup butter
- 1 pound portobello mushrooms, diced
- 1 1/2 cups port wine
- 2 cups heavy cream
- 1/4 cup chopped fresh basil

Direction

- Melt the butter in a large skillet over medium heat. Add the mushrooms; cook and stir until tender. Stir in the wine, and simmer until the liquid has reduced by 1/2. Stir in cream, and simmer again until the sauce becomes a thick gravy. Stir in the basil just before serving.

Nutrition Information

- Calories: 308 calories
- Total Fat: 27.9 g
- Cholesterol: 97 mg
- Sodium: 69 mg
- Total Carbohydrate: 5.8 g
- Protein: 2.8 g

115. Portobello Mushroom Stroganoff

"This is a rich and meaty vegetarian stroganoff made with portobello mushrooms, and served over egg noodles. It is quick to make, and tastes delicious."

Serving: 4 | Prep: 10 m | Cook: 20 m | Ready in: 30 m

Ingredients

- 3 tablespoons butter
- 1 large onion, chopped
- 3/4 pound portobello mushrooms, sliced
- 1 1/2 cups vegetable broth
- 1 1/2 cups sour cream
- 3 tablespoons all-purpose flour
- 1/4 cup chopped fresh parsley
- 8 ounces dried egg noodles

Direction

- Bring a large pot of lightly salted water to a boil. Add egg noodles, and cook until al dente, about 7 minutes. Remove from heat, drain, and set aside.
- At the same time, melt butter in a large heavy skillet over medium heat. Add onion, and cook, stirring until softened. Turn the heat up to medium-high, and add sliced mushrooms. Cook until the mushrooms are limp and browned. Remove to a bowl, and set aside.
- In the same skillet, stir in vegetable broth, being sure to stir in any browned bits off the bottom of the pan. Bring to a boil, and

cook until the mixture has reduced by 1/3. Reduce heat to low, and return the mushrooms and onion to the skillet.
- Remove the pan from the heat, stir together the sour cream and flour; then blend into the mushrooms. Return the skillet to the burner, and continue cooking over low heat, just until the sauce thickens. Stir in the parsley, and season to taste with salt and pepper. Serve over cooked egg noodles.

Nutrition Information

- Calories: 525 calories
- Total Fat: 30.1 g
- Cholesterol: 101 mg
- Sodium: 295 mg
- Total Carbohydrate: 53.3 g
- Protein: 12.8 g

116. Portobello Penne Pasta Casserole

"Portabello mushrooms, spinach, cheeses and penne combine to make a delicious casserole dish - perfect for family dinners or a party."

Serving: 8 | Prep: 15 m | Cook: 30 m | Ready in: 45 m

Ingredients

- 1 (8 ounce) package uncooked penne pasta
- 2 tablespoons vegetable oil
- 1/2 pound portobello mushrooms, thinly sliced
- 1/2 cup margarine
- 1/4 cup all-purpose flour
- 1 large clove garlic, minced
- 1/2 teaspoon dried basil
- 2 cups milk
- 2 cups shredded mozzarella cheese
- 1 (10 ounce) package frozen chopped spinach, thawed
- 1/4 cup soy sauce

Direction

- Preheat oven to 350 degrees F (175 degrees C). Lightly grease a 9x13 inch baking dish.
- Bring a large pot of lightly salted water to a boil. Place pasta in the pot, cook for 8 to 10 minutes, until al dente, and drain.
- Heat the oil in a saucepan over medium heat. Stir in the mushrooms, cook 1 minute, and set aside. Melt margarine in the saucepan. Mix in flour, garlic, and basil. Gradually mix in

milk until thickened. Stir in 1 cup cheese until melted. Remove saucepan from heat, and mix in cooked pasta, mushrooms, spinach, and soy sauce. Transfer to the prepared baking dish, and top with remaining cheese.
- Bake 20 minutes in the preheated oven, until bubbly and lightly brown.

Nutrition Information

- Calories: 380 calories
- Total Fat: 21.3 g
- Cholesterol: 23 mg
- Sodium: 811 mg
- Total Carbohydrate: 32.1 g
- Protein: 16 g

117. Portobello Pesto Egg Omelette

"Serve with whole wheat toast and you've got yourself a balanced, delicious breakfast!"

Serving: 1 | Prep: 10 m | Cook: 15 m | Ready in: 25 m

Ingredients

- 1 teaspoon olive oil
- 1 portobello mushroom cap, sliced
- 1/4 cup chopped red onion
- 4 egg whites
- 1 teaspoon water
- salt and ground black pepper to taste
- 1/4 cup shredded low-fat mozzarella cheese
- 1 teaspoon prepared pesto

Direction

- Heat the olive oil in a skillet over medium heat. Cook the portobello mushroom and red onion in the olive oil until the mushroom has softened, 3 to 5 minutes.
- Whisk the egg whites and water together in a small bowl; pour over the mushroom and onion mixture. Season the egg whites with salt and pepper. Cook, stirring occasionally, until the egg whites are no longer runny, about 5 minutes. Sprinkle the mozzarella cheese over the mixture; top with the pesto. Fold the omelette in half and continue cooking until the cheese melts, 2 to 3 minutes.

Nutrition Information

- Calories: 259 calories
- Total Fat: 12 g
- Cholesterol: 19 mg
- Sodium: 501 mg
- Total Carbohydrate: 12 g
- Protein: 28 g

118. Portobello Port Sauce for Steak

"Portobello mushrooms and port wine sauteed with sour cream and butter, to be served over pan grilled beef fillets or tenderloin. You can start this in the pan the steak was cooked in, and incorporate the steak drippings into the sauce."

Serving: 4 | Prep: 5 m | Cook: 10 m | Ready in: 15 m

Ingredients

- 1/4 pound portobello mushrooms, thinly sliced
- 3 tablespoons butter
- 1/2 cup port wine
- 2 tablespoons sour cream
- 1/2 teaspoon cornstarch
- salt and ground black pepper to taste

Direction

- Heat butter in a large heavy skillet over medium-high heat. Sauté mushrooms until soft and lightly browned, about 2 minutes. Stir in port wine, and let simmer for 2 minutes; remove from heat. In a small bowl, mix together sour cream and cornstarch. Stir into mushroom mixture until smooth. Return to heat, and stir until thickened and smooth. Season to taste with salt and pepper.

119. Portobello Pot Pie

"Flavorful vegetarian pot pie with a mushroom gravy and portabello chunk filling."

Serving: 8 | Prep: 30 m | Cook: 1 h | Ready in: 1 h 30 m

Ingredients

- 2 (9 inch) unbaked pie crusts
- 6 small red potatoes
- 3 tablespoons olive oil
- 1 cup sliced onion
- 1 cup thinly sliced fresh shiitake mushrooms
- 3 1/2 cups water
- 1/4 cup tamari or soy sauce
- 5 tablespoons rice flour
- 2 portobello mushroom caps, cut into bite size pieces
- 1 teaspoon dried thyme
- 2 teaspoons dried sage
- 2 stalks celery, chopped
- 1 carrot, cubed

Direction

- Preheat the oven to 350 degrees F (175 degrees C). Press one of the pie crusts into and up the sides of a 9 inch pie plate.
- Bring a saucepan of water to a boil. Add potatoes, and cook until tender, 10 to15 minutes. Drain, and cut into cubes. Set aside.
- Heat 1 tablespoon of olive oil in a large saucepan over low heat. Add onion and shiitake mushrooms, cover, and let the mushrooms sweat for about 7 minutes, stirring occasionally.

Pour in the water and tamari, and bring to a boil. Whisk in rice flour, stirring until there are no lumps. Allow to simmer.
- Heat remaining olive oil in a large skillet over medium-high heat. Add portobello pieces, and sauté briefly until mushrooms are browned on the outside. Add mushrooms to the gravy mixture along with the carrots, celery and potatoes. Simmer for about 10 minutes, stirring occasionally. Season with thyme and sage. Pour the mixture into the prepared crust. Cover with the other pie crust, and crimp edges to seal. Make a few slits in the top crust to vent steam.
- Bake for 40 minutes in the preheated oven, until crust is golden brown.

Nutrition Information

- Calories: 418 calories
- Total Fat: 20.4 g
- Cholesterol: 0 mg
- Sodium: 763 mg
- Total Carbohydrate: 51.9 g
- Protein: 8 g

120. Portobello Sandwiches

"Quick, juicy burgers. My friends and I eat them at least once a week!"

Serving: 4 | Prep: 8 m | Cook: 9 m | Ready in: 20 m

Ingredients

- 2 cloves garlic, minced
- 6 tablespoons olive oil
- 1/2 teaspoon dried thyme
- 2 tablespoons balsamic vinegar
- salt and pepper to taste
- 4 large portobello mushroom caps
- 4 hamburger buns
- 1 tablespoon capers
- 1/4 cup mayonnaise
- 1 tablespoon capers, drained
- 1 large tomato, sliced
- 4 leaves lettuce

Direction

- Turn on broiler, and adjust rack so it is as close to heat source as possible.
- In a medium-size mixing bowl, mix together garlic, olive oil, thyme, vinegar, salt and pepper.
- Put the mushroom caps, bottom side up, in a shallow baking pan. Brush the caps with 1/2 the dressing. Put the caps under the broiler, and cook for 5 minutes.
- Turn the caps, and brush with the remaining dressing. Broil 4 minutes. Toast the buns lightly.

- In a small bowl, mix capers and mayonnaise. Spread mayonnaise mixture on the buns, top with mushroom caps, tomato and lettuce.

Nutrition Information

- Calories: 445 calories
- Total Fat: 33.4 g
- Cholesterol: 5 mg
- Sodium: 426 mg
- Total Carbohydrate: 31.4 g
- Protein: 7.8 g

121. Portobello Stacks

"We saw these at a deli on a trip to North Carolina and copied it when we got home. It has become one of our favorite additions to any meal with beef, pork or chicken."

Serving: 4 | Prep: 20 m | Cook: 30 m | Ready in: 50 m

Ingredients

- 4 portobello mushrooms
- 1 large onion, sliced 1/4 inch thick
- 1/4 cup balsamic vinegar
- 1 eggplant, sliced into 1/2 inch rounds
- 1 tomato, sliced 1/2 inch thick
- 4 slices provolone cheese

Direction

- Marinate the mushrooms and onions in balsamic vinegar for 20 minutes.
- Preheat oven to 350 degrees F (175 degrees C).
- On a non-stick baking pan layer in four stacks: eggplant, mushroom, onion, tomato and cheese.
- Bake in preheated oven for 30 minutes, or until cheese is golden brown.

Nutrition Information

- Calories: 195 calories
- Total Fat: 8.2 g
- Cholesterol: 20 mg

- Sodium: 267 mg
- Total Carbohydrate: 21.5 g
- Protein: 12.2 g

122. Portobello Stuffed Mushroom Burger

"This mushroom is so big, you don't need beef in your burger! We don't normally add more toppings, but a slice of Vidalia® onion would be good."

Serving: 4 | Prep: 10 m | Cook: 15 m | Ready in: 25 m

Ingredients

- vegetable cooking spray
- 4 portobello mushroom caps
- 2 cups fresh spinach leaves
- 1/4 cup shredded aged Cheddar cheese
- 1/4 cup 1% cottage cheese
- 1/8 teaspoon garlic powder
- 1/8 teaspoon salt
- 4 thin, multi-grain hamburger buns

Direction

- Preheat oven to 400 degrees F (200 degrees C).
- Spray rounded ends of mushroom caps with vegetable spray and place oiled side down on baking sheet.
- Place spinach in microwave-safe bowl, sprinkle with a few drops of water, and microwave on high for one minute. Chop cooked spinach; mix with Cheddar cheese, cottage cheese, garlic powder, and salt. Spread spinach mixture onto prepared mushroom caps.
- Bake in preheated oven until the mushrooms are tender, about 12 minutes. Serve on hamburger buns.

Nutrition Information

- Calories: 195 calories
- Total Fat: 5 g
- Cholesterol: 8 mg
- Sodium: 433 mg
- Total Carbohydrate: 28.4 g
- Protein: 10.4 g

123. Portobello Wild Rice and Gizzards

"Fresh portobello mushroom sauteed with chicken gizzards and baked with wild rice - outstanding family recipe. If you need to cut down the time involved, use instant wild rice."

Serving: 6 | Prep: 15 m | Cook: 1 h 30 m | Ready in: 1 h 45 m

Ingredients

- 1 1/2 cups uncooked wild rice
- 4 1/2 cups water
- 1 pound chicken gizzards
- 1 tablespoon extra virgin olive oil
- 1/2 medium red onion, chopped
- 1 large portobello mushroom cap, chopped
- 1 clove garlic, chopped
- 1/4 cup sun-dried tomatoes
- 1 cup grated Parmesan cheese

Direction

- Place rice and water in a pot, and bring to a boil. Reduce heat to low, cover, and simmer 45 minutes.
- Preheat oven to 300 degrees F (150 degrees C). Lightly grease a medium casserole dish.
- Place gizzards in a pot with enough water to cover, and bring to a boil. Cook 15 minutes. Drain, and dice.
- Heat olive oil in a skillet, and cook the onion, mushroom, garlic, and sun-dried tomatoes until tender. Mix in the cooked gizzards, and cook until lightly browned. Transfer mixture to the

prepared casserole dish, and stir in the rice. Top with Parmesan cheese.
- Bake 20 minutes in the preheated oven, until bubbly.

Nutrition Information

- Calories: 270 calories
- Total Fat: 8.6 g
- Cholesterol: 172 mg
- Sodium: 330 mg
- Total Carbohydrate: 25.2 g
- Protein: 24.3 g

124. Pumpkin Lasagna

"I was inspired to create my own pumpkin lasagna by combining two recipes I found online. The result was well worth the effort!"

Serving: 10 | Prep: 35 m | Cook: 40 m | Ready in: 1 h 15 m

Ingredients

- 1 tablespoon minced fresh sage, divided
- 2 teaspoons salt, divided
- 1 teaspoon ground black pepper, divided
- 1/2 teaspoon ground nutmeg
- 1/2 teaspoon ground cloves
- 2 tablespoons olive oil
- 1 1/2 pounds sliced baby bella mushrooms
- 1 large onion, diced
- 2 cloves garlic, minced
- 3 cups pumpkin puree, divided
- 1 1/2 cups heavy whipping cream, divided
- 1 1/2 cups grated Parmesan cheese
- cooking spray
- 12 lasagna noodles
- 1 cup ricotta cheese
- 1 cup shredded mozzarella cheese
- 1 dash ground nutmeg
- 1 dash ground cloves
- 2 tablespoons butter, cut in small pieces

Direction

- Preheat oven to 400 degrees F (200 degrees C).

- Mix sage, salt, black pepper, 1/2 teaspoon nutmeg, and 1/2 teaspoon cloves together in a small bowl to make a spice blend.
- Heat olive oil in a large skillet over medium-high heat. Add mushrooms, onion, garlic, and 1/2 of the spice blend; cook and stir until mushrooms are tender and all moisture has evaporated, about 5 minutes.
- Combine 2 cups pumpkin puree, 3/4 cup heavy cream, 1/2 cup Parmesan cheese, and remaining spice blend in a bowl.
- Grease a 9x13-inch baking pan with cooking spray. Arrange 4 lasagna noodles in the bottom so they slightly overlap. Cover with 1/2 of the pumpkin mixture and 1/2 of the mushroom mixture. Dot with 1/2 cup ricotta; sprinkle 1/2 cup mozzarella cheese on top. Repeat layers once more. Place remaining 4 noodles on top.
- Combine remaining 1 cup pumpkin puree, remaining 3/4 cup heavy cream, 1 dash nutmeg, and 1 dash cloves. Spread on top of noodles. Sprinkle remaining 1 cup Parmesan cheese on top. Dot with butter. Cover with aluminum foil.
- Bake in the preheated oven for 20 minutes. Uncover and bake until bubbly, about 15 minutes more.

Nutrition Information

- Calories: 401 calories
- Total Fat: 24.7 g
- Cholesterol: 73 mg
- Sodium: 932 mg
- Total Carbohydrate: 33 g
- Protein: 15.1 g

125. Roasted Portabello Mushrooms with Blue Cheese

"Meaty portabellos are topped with blue cheese. Great as an appetizer, or build a burger with crusty rolls, red onion slices, lettuce and tomato. I chopped the mushroom stems, sauteed them, and added them to the hamburger patties we barbecued. Yum, yum!"

Serving: 2 | Prep: 15 m | Cook: 35 m | Ready in: 50 m

Ingredients

- 2 portobello mushroom caps
- 1 tablespoon balsamic vinegar reduction, or to taste
- freshly ground black pepper
- 3 tablespoons crumbled blue cheese
- 1 tablespoon roasted pine nuts, or to taste
- 1/4 teaspoon crushed garlic

Direction

- Preheat oven to 425 degrees F (220 degrees C).
- Place mushroom caps, tops facing down, on a baking sheet. Drizzle balsamic vinegar on each cap and sprinkle black pepper over vinegar.
- Bake in the preheated oven until tender and fragrant, about 25 minutes. Sprinkle blue cheese, pine nuts, and garlic on each cap. Continue roasting until cheese melts, about 10 minutes more.

Nutrition Information

- Calories: 105 calories
- Total Fat: 6.1 g
- Cholesterol: 9 mg
- Sodium: 186 mg
- Total Carbohydrate: 8.2 g
- Protein: 6.6 g

126. Roasted Portobello Mushroom Fettuccine

"This is my version of a recipe I encountered while traveling. It was so good that I had to recreate it at home for my family. This is really good served with crusty bread and a nice riesling. Enjoy!"

Serving: 4 | Prep: 25 m | Cook: 30 m | Ready in: 55 m

Ingredients

- 4 portobello mushroom caps
- 1/4 cup balsamic vinegar
- 1 red bell pepper
- 1 yellow bell pepper
- 8 ounces uncooked fettuccine pasta
- 1 tablespoon olive oil
- 1 tablespoon butter
- 1/4 pound fresh asparagus, trimmed and cut into 1-inch pieces
- 1 clove garlic, minced
- 1 teaspoon Italian herb seasoning
- 1 pinch crushed red pepper flakes, or to taste
- salt and ground black pepper to taste

Direction

- Place portobello mushroom caps into a large resealable plastic bag and pour in balsamic vinegar. Seal the bag and shake several times to coat mushrooms with vinegar; set aside to marinate.
- Set an oven rack about 6 inches from broiler's heat source, and preheat oven's broiler.

- Line a baking sheet with aluminum foil.
- Cut red and yellow bell peppers in half from top to bottom; remove stems, seeds, and ribs. Place the peppers cut sides down onto the prepared baking sheet.
- Cook under the preheated broiler until the skin of the peppers has blackened and blistered, about 5 minutes.
- Place the blackened peppers into a bowl and tightly seal with plastic wrap. Allow the peppers to steam as they cool, about 20 minutes. Once cool, remove the skins and discard. Chop roasted peppers.
- Turn oven's temperature to 500 degrees F (260 degrees C).
- Remove portobello mushroom caps from bag, shake off excess vinegar, and arrange onto a baking sheet.
- Roast mushrooms until tender and they give off their liquid, 5 to 8 minutes. Remove mushrooms from oven and set aside. Chop mushrooms when cool enough to handle.
- Fill a large pot with lightly salted water and bring to a boil. Stir in fettuccine and return to a boil. Cook the pasta until tender but still slightly firm, about 8 minutes; drain.
- Heat olive oil and butter in a large skillet over medium heat until butter has melted; cook and stir asparagus with garlic, Italian seasoning, crushed red pepper flakes, salt, and black pepper until asparagus is tender but still bright green, about 3 minutes.
- Mix portobello mushrooms and roasted peppers into asparagus mixture and toss fettuccine with the vegetables until combined.

Nutrition Information

- Calories: 320 calories
- Total Fat: 8 g
- Cholesterol: 8 mg
- Sodium: 37 mg
- Total Carbohydrate: 54.1 g

- Protein: 11.6 g

127. Roasted Portobello Red Pepper and Arugula Salad for One

"This is my super easy version of a salad I had at a restaurant in Chicago. I usually only cook for one, but this would be easy to make in a larger batch for more people."

Serving: 1 | Prep: 15 m | Cook: 30 m | Ready in: 45 m

Ingredients

- 1 portobello mushroom, stem removed
- 1 tablespoon olive oil
- 1 teaspoon red wine vinegar
- 1 clove garlic, thinly sliced
- 1/4 shallot, thinly sliced
- salt and pepper to taste
- 1/2 roasted red pepper, cut into strips
- 3 cups arugula leaves
- 1 ounce grated Romano cheese
- 1 tablespoon Greek salad dressing

Direction

- Preheat oven to 425 degrees F (220 degrees C). Line a baking sheet with a piece of aluminum foil.
- Brush the mushroom on both sides with olive oil and place gill-side up onto the baking sheet. Drizzle with any remaining olive oil, and the red wine vinegar. Sprinkle with sliced garlic and shallot; season to taste with salt and pepper. Top with the piece

of roasted red pepper, and wrap the foil tightly around the mushroom.
- Bake in preheated oven until the mushroom is tender, about 30 minutes.
- Toss the arugula with Romano cheese and salad dressing. Place onto a plate and top with the hot mushroom and pepper. Dig in!

Nutrition Information

- Calories: 352 calories
- Total Fat: 27.5 g
- Cholesterol: 29 mg
- Sodium: 644 mg
- Total Carbohydrate: 15.2 g
- Protein: 14.5 g

128. Roasted Vegetable Orzo

"This is a recipe I made up with all of the wonderful summer vegetables in season. Serve it with chicken or all on its own!"

Serving: 4 | Prep: 25 m | Cook: 20 m | Ready in: 45 m

Ingredients

- 1 zucchini, sliced
- 1 summer squash, sliced
- 1 red onion, cut into chunks
- 1 pound asparagus, cut into 1-inch pieces
- 1 pound portobello mushrooms, thickly sliced
- 4 cloves garlic, minced
- 2 tablespoons olive oil
- 1 pinch white sugar
- salt and black pepper to taste
- 4 cubes chicken bouillon
- 1/4 cup dry white wine
- 1 (16 ounce) package orzo pasta
- 2 tablespoons grated Parmesan cheese

Direction

- Preheat oven to 450 degrees F (230 degrees C).
- Place the zucchini, squash, onion, asparagus, and mushrooms in a large bowl; add in garlic, olive oil and sugar, and stir gently to coat vegetables. Spread vegetables in a single layer on a baking sheet, and sprinkle with salt and pepper.
- Roast vegetables until tender, 20 to 25 minutes.

- Meanwhile, bring a large pot of lightly salted water to boil. Add bouillon cubes, wine, and orzo, and cook until al dente, about 8 to 10 minutes. Drain. Stir in roasted vegetables and Parmesan cheese, and serve warm.

Nutrition Information

- Calories: 621 calories
- Total Fat: 11.4 g
- Cholesterol: 3 mg
- Sodium: 1042 mg
- Total Carbohydrate: 104.5 g
- Protein: 24.9 g

129. Roasted Vegetables with Walnuts Basil and Balsamic Vinaigrette

"This colorful veggie dish with red and orange bell peppers, red onions, mushrooms, sugar snap peas and squash is tossed with balsamic vinegar and chopped walnuts and topped with fresh basil."

Serving: 5 | Prep: 15 m | Cook: 10 m | Ready in: 25 m

Ingredients

- 1/2 small red bell pepper, cut into 1-inch cubes
- 1/2 small orange bell pepper, cut into 1-inch cubes
- 1/4 medium red onion, cut into 1-inch cubes, separated
- 4 ounces baby portabella mushrooms, halved
- 1 tablespoon extra virgin olive oil
- 1/4 teaspoon sea salt
- 3/4 cup sugar snap peas
- 1 small zucchini, sliced 1/4-inch thick
- 1 small yellow summer squash, sliced 1/4-inch thick
- 2 cloves garlic, minced
- 2 teaspoons balsamic vinegar
- 2 tablespoons fresh snipped basil
- 1/2 cup California walnuts, coarsely chopped

Direction

- Preheat oven to 400 degrees F. Place bell peppers, onion and mushrooms in a large bowl and toss with olive oil and salt.

Place in a single layer on a large baking sheet, making sure not to crowd vegetables. Cook for 10 minutes.
- Add snap peas, zucchini, yellow squash and garlic and stir lightly. Top with walnuts and cook for 5 to 10 minutes more or until all vegetables are crisp-tender and walnuts are toasted.
- Drizzle with balsamic and toss well. Sprinkle with basil.

Nutrition Information

- Calories: 137 calories
- Total Fat: 10.5 g
- Cholesterol: 0 mg
- Sodium: 94 mg
- Total Carbohydrate: 8.8 g
- Protein: 3.9 g

130. Root Veggie Casserole

"As a vegetarian, I'm always looking for interesting ways to combine vegetables. The flavorful gravy in this dish comes from the mushroom-soy sauce-miso combination. Eat alone or as a side dish. Enjoy!"

Serving: 2 | Prep: 20 m | Cook: 40 m | Ready in: 1 h

Ingredients

- 1 tablespoon butter
- 1 small onion, diced
- 1 large portobello mushroom, cut into chunks
- 1 tablespoon soy sauce
- 1/2 cup hot water
- 1/3 cube low-sodium vegetable bouillon
- 1 large potato, cut into cubes
- 1 kohlrabi bulb, cut into cubes
- 1 carrot, thinly sliced
- 1 bay leaf
- 1/2 teaspoon parsley flakes
- 1/3 teaspoon seasoned salt (such as Herbamare®)
- ground black pepper to taste
- 2 tablespoons miso paste

Direction

- Preheat oven to 400 degrees F (200 degrees C).
- Melt butter in a skillet over medium heat. Cook and stir onion in butter for 1 minute. Stir mushroom into onion; continue cooking and stirring until mushroom softens, about 3 minutes more.

- Pour soy sauce over mushroom mixture; cook for 1 minute and remove from heat.
- Pour hot water into a casserole dish. Stir bouillon in the hot water to dissolve. Mix potato, kohlrabi, and carrot in the bouillon mixture. Add mushroom mixture to potato mixture; stir. Top with bay leaf, parsley, seasoned salt, and black pepper. Stir again to evenly distribute seasoning.
- Divide miso into 4 portions; place atop vegetable mixture.
- Bake in the preheated oven for 20 minutes, stir, and continue cooking until vegetables are tender, about 15 minutes more.

Nutrition Information

- Calories: 291 calories
- Total Fat: 7.4 g
- Cholesterol: 15 mg
- Sodium: 1818 mg
- Total Carbohydrate: 51.6 g
- Protein: 7.9 g

131. Sauceless Garden Lasagna

"This is a tasty lasagna that I developed to help use up the abundance of tomatoes and zucchini from my garden. I didn't have any pasta sauce on hand, so I just added the herbs to the vegetable mixture. Even my daughter and her picky friends ate it!"

Serving: 6 | Prep: 20 m | Cook: 45 m | Ready in: 1 h 5 m

Ingredients

- 1 medium zucchini, halved lengthwise and sliced
- 1/3 cup chopped red onion
- 1 cup shredded mozzarella cheese, divided
- 1/2 cup crumbled feta cheese
- 2 portobello mushrooms, sliced
- 4 cups fresh baby spinach
- 1/4 cup chopped fresh basil
- 1 tablespoon chopped fresh oregano
- 3 cloves garlic, minced
- 3 tablespoons olive oil
- 1/4 cup balsamic vinegar
- 1 teaspoon sugar
- 1/2 teaspoon salt
- 1/4 teaspoon freshly ground black pepper
- 1 (8 ounce) package no-boil lasagna noodles
- 9 roma (plum) tomatoes, thinly sliced

Direction

- Preheat the oven to 350 degrees F (175 degrees C). Lightly coat a 9x9 inch baking dish with cooking spray.

- In a large bowl, toss together the zucchini, mushrooms, spinach, garlic, red onion, 1/2 cup mozzarella cheese, and feta cheese. Drizzle with olive oil and balsamic vinegar, and stir in basil, oregano, sugar, salt and pepper. Stir the mixture until evenly blended.
- Place a layer of lasagna noodles into the bottom of the prepared pan. Make a layer of tomato slices over the noodles. Spread a generous amount of the spinach mixture over the tomatoes. Don't worry, it shrinks a lot while cooking. Lay slices of tomatoes over the spinach mixture, then another layer of noodles. Start with another layer of tomatoes on top of the noodles, and repeat layering until the dish is heaped with lasagna, ending with the vegetable mixture. Sprinkle remaining cheese on the top.
- Bake for 35 to 45 minutes in the preheated oven, until noodles, and vegetables are tender. Let stand for a few minutes to set, then slice and serve.

Nutrition Information

- Calories: 286 calories
- Total Fat: 15.5 g
- Cholesterol: 32 mg
- Sodium: 576 mg
- Total Carbohydrate: 25.3 g
- Protein: 12.9 g

132. Sausage Mushroom and Cranberry Tart

"This tasty tart with sausage, dried cranberries, lots of mushrooms, cheese and eggs will be the star of your holiday brunch."

Serving: 8 | Prep: 30 m | Cook: 30 m | Ready in: 1 h

Ingredients

- 1/2 (14.1 ounce) package refrigerated pie crust
- 1 (9.6 ounce) package Jimmy Dean® Original Hearty Turkey Sausage Crumbles
- 3 tablespoons butter
- 1 1/2 cups sliced fresh button mushrooms
- 1 1/2 cups sliced fresh baby portobello mushrooms
- 2 eggs, lightly beaten
- 1 1/2 cups shredded Gruyere or Swiss cheese
- 3/4 cup dried cranberries, divided
- 1/2 cup whipping cream
- 3 tablespoons minced fresh parsley
- 2 green onions, thinly sliced

Direction

- Preheat oven to 450 degrees F. Press pie crust onto bottom and up side of 9-inch fluted tart pan with removable bottom; trim edge, reserving trimmings. Prick bottom of crust with fork. Bake 10-12 minutes or until golden brown. Cool. Reduce heat to 375 degrees F.

- Cook sausage in large skillet over medium heat 4-5 minutes or until hot stirring frequently. Remove from skillet; set aside.
- Melt butter in same skillet. Add mushrooms; cook 3 minutes or until tender, stirring occasionally. Place in large bowl. Add eggs, cheese, 1/2 cup cranberries, cream, parsley and sausage; mix well. Pour into tart shell.
- Roll out reserved pie crust trimmings on lightly floured surface. Use cookie cutters to cut into decorative shapes; arrange over filling.
- Bake 25-30 minutes or until knife inserted in center comes out clean. Top with onions and remaining cranberries. Cut into 8 wedges to serve.

Nutrition Information

- Calories: 453 calories
- Total Fat: 35.2 g
- Cholesterol: 111 mg
- Sodium: 375 mg
- Total Carbohydrate: 22.2 g
- Protein: 13.1 g

133. Sauteed Mushrooms Quick and Simple

"Delicious as a side, appetizer, part of a salad, or even just a snack! How French of you!"

Serving: 2 | Prep: 10 m | Cook: 10 m | Ready in: 20 m

Ingredients

- 1 tablespoon unsalted butter
- 2 tablespoons olive oil
- 1 cup chopped Portobello mushrooms
- 2 teaspoons dried oregano
- 1 teaspoon garlic powder
- 1 teaspoon steak seasoning rub (optional)

Direction

- Heat butter and olive oil in a skillet over medium heat. Stir mushrooms in the oil and butter until well coated. Sprinkle oregano, garlic powder, and steak seasoning on mushrooms; stir to coat. Cook and stir mushrooms until lightly browned, about 5 minutes.

Nutrition Information

- Calories: 194 calories
- Total Fat: 19.6 g
- Cholesterol: 15 mg
- Sodium: 503 mg

- Total Carbohydrate: 4.9 g
- Protein: 1.7 g

134. Sauteed Portobellos and Spinach

"Tender portobello mushrooms and spinach are simmered with Parmesan cheese, wine and seasoning. Unique, easy, and extremely tasty side dish! Excellent with a steak and baked potato dinner."

Serving: 4 | Prep: 10 m | Cook: 10 m | Ready in: 20 m

Ingredients

- 3 tablespoons butter
- 2 large portobello mushrooms, sliced
- 1 (10 ounce) package frozen chopped spinach, thawed and drained
- 1/4 teaspoon dried basil
- 1/4 teaspoon salt
- 1/4 teaspoon black pepper
- 1 clove garlic, chopped
- 2 tablespoons dry red wine
- 1/4 cup grated Parmesan cheese

Direction

- Melt butter in a large skillet or sauté pan over medium heat. Sauté mushrooms, spinach, basil, salt, pepper and garlic until mushrooms are tender and spinach is heated through.
- Pour in wine and reduce heat to low; simmer 1 minute. Stir in Parmesan cheese and serve.

Nutrition Information

- Calories: 146 calories
- Total Fat: 11 g
- Cholesterol: 28 mg
- Sodium: 359 mg
- Total Carbohydrate: 6.6 g
- Protein: 6.6 g

135. Savannahs Best Marinated Portobello Mushrooms

"This is simple and tasty with some rice or couscous and a colorful vegetable; I made a bell pepper, garbanzo, sesame salad. Mmmm, good as a burger too."

Serving: 2 | Prep: 10 m | Cook: 33 m | Ready in: 1 h

Ingredients

- 1/2 cup cooking wine
- 1 tablespoon olive oil
- 2 tablespoons dark soy sauce
- 2 tablespoons balsamic vinegar
- 2 cloves garlic, minced
- 2 large portobello mushroom caps

Direction

- Preheat oven to 400 degrees F (200 degrees C).
- In a baking dish, mix the wine, olive oil, soy sauce, balsamic vinegar, and garlic. Place mushroom caps upside down in the marinade, and marinate 15 minutes.
- Cover dish, and transfer to the preheated oven. Bake 25 minutes. Turn mushrooms and continue baking 8 minutes.

Nutrition Information

- Calories: 112 calories
- Total Fat: 6.8 g
- Cholesterol: 0 mg

- Sodium: 1286 mg
- Total Carbohydrate: 4.5 g
- Protein: 1.3 g

136. Savory Portobello Mushroom Burgers

"This is a quick, easy, and light alternative to the regular beef burger. Many meat eaters I know love these! Can be topped with mayo, tomatoes, and shredded old Cheddar or Monterey Jack cheese. I prefer to top them with roasted red peppers and goat cheese."

Serving: 4 | Prep: 15 m | Cook: 10 m | Ready in: 35 m

Ingredients

- 2 tablespoons olive oil
- 2 tablespoons balsamic vinegar
- 1 tablespoon Dijon mustard
- 2 cloves garlic, minced
- 1/2 teaspoon Worcestershire sauce (optional)
- 1 pinch salt and ground black pepper
- 4 large portobello mushrooms, stems removed
- 4 kaiser rolls, split

Direction

- Preheat grill for medium-high heat and lightly oil the grate.
- Whisk olive oil, balsamic vinegar, Dijon mustard, garlic, Worcestershire sauce, salt, and pepper in a bowl. Brush the mixture over the tops and bottoms of the mushrooms; let stand for 10 minutes.
- Grill mushrooms on the preheated grill with the cover closed until mushrooms are browned and tender, about 10 minutes, turning once. Serve on kaiser rolls.

Nutrition Information

- Calories: 188 calories
- Total Fat: 8.5 g
- Cholesterol: 0 mg
- Sodium: 321 mg
- Total Carbohydrate: 23.7 g
- Protein: 4.1 g

137. Savory Swiss Chard with Portobellos

"Absolutely delicious way to make Swiss chard. It has a comforting flavor and beautiful presentation. The colors are amazing and I often prepare this for family for Christmas dinner paired with standing rib roast and mashed potatoes and gravy. A huge hit in my family!"

Serving: 8 | Prep: 20 m | Cook: 35 m | Ready in: 1 h

Ingredients

- 2 tablespoons olive oil
- 1 teaspoon crushed red pepper
- 1 clove garlic, crushed and chopped
- 1 (8 ounce) package portobello mushrooms, stemmed and cut into 1/2-inch wide by 2-inch long pieces
- 1 leek, chopped
- 1 cup chicken broth
- 1 bunch Swiss chard, trimmed and chopped
- 2 cups grated Parmesan cheese

Direction

- Heat the olive oil in a large pot over medium-high heat. Stir in the red pepper, garlic, and portobello mushrooms. Cook and stir until the mushroom has softened and begun to release its liquid, 3 to 5 minutes. Stir in the leek, and continue cooking until the leek has softened, about 5 minutes.
- Stir in the chicken broth and Swiss chard. Bring to a boil, then reduce heat to medium-low. Cover, and simmer until the chard leaves have wilted, about 10 minutes. Remove the lid, and

continue cooking until the chard is tender and most of the liquid has evaporated, about 5 minutes. Sprinkle with the Parmesan cheese; let stand until melted.

Nutrition Information

- Calories: 139 calories
- Total Fat: 9.4 g
- Cholesterol: 18 mg
- Sodium: 490 mg
- Total Carbohydrate: 5.3 g
- Protein: 9.3 g

138. Scallop Topped Portabello Mushrooms

"This is a nice dish to serve guests for dinner or even at a special lunch. It's extremely presentable and will wow everybody at the table. Be sure to use the Japanese mayonnaise recommended in this recipe, not American-style mayonnaise because the flavors are entirely different. Japanese mayonnaise is more flat/sour tasting while American-style mayonnaise is extremely sweet. American-style mayonnaise will ruin the recipe completely."

Serving: 4 | Prep: 15 m | Cook: 20 m | Ready in: 35 m

Ingredients

- 3 tablespoons butter, divided
- 4 large portobello mushrooms, stems removed
- 1 dash garlic powder
- 1 tablespoon butter
- 2 pounds scallops
- 1 cup Japanese mayonnaise, such as Kewpie brand
- 1/2 teaspoon chili-garlic sauce, or to taste
- 2 tablespoons green onions, chopped

Direction

- Melt 1/4 of the 3 tablespoon of butter in a skillet over medium-high heat, add a mushroom cap, and cook on both sides until completely soft to the center, about 3 minutes. Repeat with remaining butter and mushrooms, and place the cooked mushrooms upside-down on an aluminum foil-lined baking sheet; sprinkle with garlic powder.

- Preheat the oven's broiler and set the oven rack at about 6 inches from the heat source.
- Melt the remaining 1 tablespoon of butter in a skillet over medium-high heat. Add the scallops, and cook until just firm, and lightly browned on both sides. Divide scallops among mushroom caps. Stir together mayonnaise and chili sauce in a small bowl, and spoon over the scallops.
- Broil until the mayonnaise has developed brown patches and is hot, 3 to 5 minutes. Sprinkle with green onions to serve.

Nutrition Information

- Calories: 823 calories
- Total Fat: 57.5 g
- Cholesterol: 189 mg
- Sodium: 1084 mg
- Total Carbohydrate: 18.4 g
- Protein: 60.5 g

139. Seafood Lasagna II

"This super rich, Alfredo based seafood lasagna is a huge hit in our family. It takes a while to prepare, but it is well worth it!"

Serving: 12 | Prep: 30 m | Cook: 1 h 30 m | Ready in: 2 h

Ingredients

- 1 (16 ounce) package lasagna noodles
- 2 tablespoons olive oil
- 1 clove garlic, minced
- 1 pound baby portobello mushrooms, sliced
- 2 (16 ounce) jars Alfredo-style pasta sauce
- 1 pound shrimp, peeled and deveined
- 1 pound bay scallops
- 1 pound imitation crabmeat, chopped
- 20 ounces ricotta cheese
- 1 egg
- black pepper
- 6 cups shredded Italian cheese blend

Direction

- Preheat oven to 350 degrees F (175 degrees C). Bring a large pot of lightly salted water to a boil. Add pasta and cook for 8 to 10 minutes or until al dente; drain.
- Heat oil in a large saucepan over medium heat. Sautee garlic and mushrooms until tender. Pour in 2 jars Alfredo sauce. Stir in shrimp, scallops and crabmeat. Simmer 5 to 10 minutes, or until heated through. In a medium bowl, combine ricotta cheese, egg and pepper.

- In a 9x13 inch baking dish, layer noodles, ricotta mixture, Alfredo mixture and shredded cheese. Repeat layers until all ingredients are used, ensuring that there is shredded cheese for the top.
- Bake uncovered in preheated oven for 45 minutes. Cover, and bake 15 minutes.

Nutrition Information

- Calories: 764 calories
- Total Fat: 46 g
- Cholesterol: 183 mg
- Sodium: 1726 mg
- Total Carbohydrate: 44.4 g
- Protein: 45.7 g

140. Seared Salmon with IndianInspired Cream Sauce

"Salmon fillets smothered in a rich mushroom cream sauce and garnished with parsley, green onions slices, and lemon slices. The sauce has fennel, garlic, mushrooms, saffron and curry."

Serving: 4 | Prep: 45 m | Cook: 25 m | Ready in: 1 h 10 m

Ingredients

- 4 (6 ounce) fillets fresh salmon
- salt and black pepper to taste
- 1 tablespoon butter
- 2 medium onions, diced
- 8 cloves garlic, minced
- 1 cup chopped portobello mushrooms
- 1 cup fresh porcini mushrooms, cleaned and sliced
- 1/2 cup diced fennel bulb
- 1/2 cup diced celery
- 1 teaspoon curry powder
- 1/2 teaspoon saffron
- 2 cups chicken broth
- 1 cup heavy cream
- 1 tablespoon butter
- 4 sprigs chopped fresh parsley for garnish
- 4 lemon slices for garnish
- 2 tablespoons thinly sliced green onion for garnish

Direction

- Season each fillet with salt and pepper; set aside.

- Melt 1 tablespoon butter in a large skillet over medium heat. Stir in onions and cook until they soften and turn translucent, 5 to 7 minutes. Add garlic and cook 1 minute more. Combine mushrooms, fennel, and celery with onions and cook until vegetables have softened, about 5 to 7 minutes. Season with curry powder, saffron, salt and pepper to taste; cook 2 more minutes. Pour in chicken broth and cook 5 minutes longer, stirring occasionally. Stir in heavy cream and simmer 5 minutes.
- Meanwhile, melt 1 tablespoon butter in a large skillet over medium heat and place salmon fillets in pan, skin side down. Turn up heat to high to sear fillets; cooking two minutes on each side.
- Prepare serving platter by spooning mushroom sauce over the bottom. Place salmon fillets on top, drizzling additional sauce over fish. Garnish with parsley, lemon slices, and green onions.

Nutrition Information

- Calories: 599 calories
- Total Fat: 44.7 g
- Cholesterol: 182 mg
- Sodium: 665 mg
- Total Carbohydrate: 16.5 g
- Protein: 34.3 g

141. Shrimp and Portobello Mushroom Fettuccine

"This is an easy dish and can be made with different variations. It's also good with chicken breasts, or other seafood such as crawfish tails, scallions or crab meat. Also great with angel hair pasta instead of fettuccine noodles. Sliced white mushrooms can be used if preferred. Hope you enjoy as much as my family does!"

Serving: 6 | Prep: 30 m | Cook: 30 m | Ready in: 1 h

Ingredients

- 1 (16 ounce) package dry fettuccini noodles
- 3/4 cup butter, divided
- 1 pound baby portobello mushrooms, sliced
- 1 large onion, chopped
- 3 cloves garlic, minced
- 4 ounces cream cheese
- 2 tablespoons all-purpose flour
- 1 pint whipping cream
- 1/2 cup freshly grated Parmesan cheese, divided
- 2 pounds medium shrimp, peeled and deveined
- 1 tablespoon Cajun seasoning
- salt and pepper to taste
- 1/2 cup green onions, chopped

Direction

- Bring a large pot of lightly salted water to boil. Add pasta, and cook until al dente, about 8 to 10 minutes. Drain, and set aside.

- Meanwhile, heat 1/4 cup butter in a large skillet over medium heat. Stir in mushrooms, and cook until soft. Remove mushrooms, and set aside. Wipe out skillet.
- Heat 1/2 cup butter in the skillet over medium-high heat. Stir in onions, and cook until soft and translucent. Stir in garlic, and cook 1 minute. Add cream cheese, and cook until melted.
- Reduce heat to medium low, and stir in flour, whipping cream, and 1/4 cup Parmesan cheese. Stir in shrimp, and season with Cajun seasoning, salt, and pepper. Cook until shrimp are pink and sauce thickens, about 3 minutes. Remove from heat. Fold mushrooms, green onions, and fettuccine into sauce. Sprinkle with remaining 1/4 cup Parmesan, and serve.

Nutrition Information

- Calories: 1050 calories
- Total Fat: 65.5 g
- Cholesterol: 426 mg
- Sodium: 823 mg
- Total Carbohydrate: 69.1 g
- Protein: 49.5 g

142. Slow Cooker Cornish Hens

"This is my fiance's favorite slow cooker meal of mine.

I usually serve it with the veggies over wild rice. You can turn this recipe for 2 into 4 by splitting the hens lengthwise after cooking."

Serving: 2 | Prep: 20 m | Cook: 4 h | Ready in: 4 h 20 m

Ingredients

- 2 Cornish game hens
- 1 (10.75 ounce) can golden mushroom soup (such as Campbell's®), divided
- 2 cups chopped baby portobello mushrooms
- 1 (7 ounce) jar pimento-stuffed green olives, drained and chopped
- 1 large zucchini, chopped
- 1 teaspoon garlic salt

Direction

- Coat the hens with about 1/4 of the mushroom soup.
- Mix the remaining mushroom soup with mushrooms, olives, zucchini, and garlic salt in a bowl. Stuff the mixture inside the hens. Arrange hens, breast sides up, in the slow cooker. Spoon any remaining soup mixture over the hens.
- Cook the hens in the slow cooker on High for 4 hours.

Nutrition Information

- Calories: 851 calories

- Total Fat: 57.6 g
- Cholesterol: 308 mg
- Sodium: 4201 mg
- Total Carbohydrate: 24.5 g
- Protein: 59.5 g

143. South Dakota Wild Mushroom Dip

"This tailgate favorite involves minimal prep work and packs a ton of melty goodness �all ready in time for kickoff. Three kinds of mushrooms �shiitake, oyster and portobello �bring an earthy flavor to the Monterey Jack cheese and McCormick® Brown Gravy Mix base. (Morel hunting is very popular in South Dakota!) Try it with onion rings, fries or crusty bread."

Serving: 12 | Prep: 5 m | Cook: 20 m | Ready in: 25 m

Ingredients

- 1 tablespoon butter
- 1 cup sliced mushrooms, such as oyster, portobello or shiitake
- 1/4 cup chopped onion
- 1/2 cup milk
- 1/2 cup water
- 1 (.87 ounce) package McCormick® Brown Gravy Mix
- 1 cup shredded Monterey Jack cheese, divided

Direction

- Preheat oven to 350 degrees F. Melt butter in large skillet on medium-high heat. Add mushrooms and onion; cook and stir until softened.
- Mix milk, water and Gravy Mix in small bowl. Stir into mushroom mixture. Cook on medium heat until gravy comes to boil, stirring frequently. Reduce heat to simmer. Stir in 3/4 cup of the cheese. Simmer 1 to 2 minutes or until cheese is melted and gravy has thickened slightly.

- Spoon into 1-quart baking dish. Sprinkle with remaining 1/4 cup cheese.
- Bake 5 to 10 minutes or until cheese is melted. Serve with onion rings, fries or crusty bread.

Nutrition Information

- Calories: 59 calories
- Total Fat: 4.2 g
- Cholesterol: 12 mg
- Sodium: 180 mg
- Total Carbohydrate: 2.3 g
- Protein: 2.9 g

144. Spaghetti Bolognese

"A Bolognese recipe with a real personality. It's been a favorite of family and friends for years and is easy but delicious."

Serving: 6 | Prep: 15 m | Cook: 45 m | Ready in: 1 h

Ingredients

- 2 pounds lean ground beef
- 1 large white onion, diced
- 1 large portobello mushroom, diced, or more to taste
- 2 (14.5 ounce) cans petite diced tomatoes
- 3 (10 ounce) cans condensed tomato soup
- 1/2 cup Worcestershire sauce
- 1 1/2 tablespoons garlic and herb seasoning blend (such as Mrs. Dash®)
- 1 tablespoon lemon juice
- 1 tablespoon minced garlic
- 1/4 cup chili powder (optional)
- 3 tablespoons Cajun seasoning (optional)
- 1/2 teaspoon dried basil
- 1/4 teaspoon vanilla extract
- 1/4 teaspoon black pepper
- 1/2 teaspoon salt
- 1 (16 ounce) package spaghetti
- 1 1/2 tablespoons extra-virgin olive oil

Direction

- Cook the ground beef in a large pot over high heat, stirring quickly and constantly until completely browned 7 to 10

minutes. Stir the onion into the beef; cook and stir until the onion begins to turn translucent, about 5 minutes more. Drain excess grease from meat mixture. Add the mushroom to the mixture; allow to cook until it begins to soften, 1 to 2 minutes. Pour the diced tomatoes and tomato soup into the pot, stir, reduce heat to medium, and bring the mixture to a simmer.
- Add the Worcestershire sauce, garlic and herb seasoning blend, lemon juice, garlic, chili powder, Cajun seasoning, basil, vanilla extract, black pepper, and salt to the mixture, stirring each into the mixture before adding the next. Reduce heat to low and allow the mixture to simmer for 30 minutes.
- Bring a large pot of lightly salted water to a rolling boil. Add the spaghetti and olive oil to the pot and cook the pasta at a boil until cooked through yet firm to the bite, about 12 minutes. Drain. Top with the Bolognese sauce to serve.

Nutrition Information

- Calories: 782 calories
- Total Fat: 26.2 g
- Cholesterol: 105 mg
- Sodium: 2277 mg
- Total Carbohydrate: 91.1 g
- Protein: 43.9 g

145. Spicy Chicken Orecchiette

"Cute orecchiette pasta with fresh vegetables, grilled pulled chicken, and lots of spice. Delicious!"

Serving: 4 | Prep: 30 m | Cook: 25 m | Ready in: 1 h 10 m

Ingredients

- 2 skinless, boneless chicken breast halves
- 1 cup uncooked orecchiette pasta
- 1 cup tomato pasta sauce
- 1/2 cup broccolini, cut into 1 inch pieces
- 1/2 (14.5 ounce) can stewed tomatoes, drained
- 1/3 cup sliced portobello mushrooms
- 2 tablespoons minced garlic
- 2 teaspoons crushed red pepper flakes

Direction

- Preheat grill for medium heat and lightly oil the grate.
- Grill chicken breast halves until they show dark grill marks and are no longer pink inside, about 5 minutes per side. Let the chicken breasts cool, then place into a bowl and coarsely shred with 2 forks.
- Bring a large pot of lightly salted water to a boil. Cook orecchiette pasta in the boiling water, stirring occasionally until cooked through but firm to the bite, 5 to 8 minutes. Drain and return pasta to pot.
- Stir chicken breast meat, pasta sauce, broccolini, stewed tomatoes, portobello mushrooms, garlic, and red pepper flakes into the cooked pasta. Place over medium heat and cook,

stirring frequently, until the mushrooms and broccolini are cooked through and tender, 5 to 10 minutes.

Nutrition Information

- Calories: 223 calories
- Total Fat: 3.8 g
- Cholesterol: 35 mg
- Sodium: 402 mg
- Total Carbohydrate: 30.2 g
- Protein: 17.4 g

146. Spicy Sweetbreads

"Sweetbreads are tasty and easily digested. I couldn't find a spicy recipe so invented this simple, delicious dish. The sliced jalapeno gives a lovely bite of heat."

Serving: 4 | Prep: 15 m | Cook: 34 m | Ready in: 1 h 49 m

Ingredients

- 16 ounces lamb sweetbreads
- 7 tablespoons butter, divided
- 1/2 lemon, juiced
- salt to taste
- 2 large portobello mushrooms, diced
- 1 tablespoon all-purpose flour
- 1 teaspoon ground paprika
- 1/2 teaspoon cayenne pepper
- 1 cup warmed milk, or to taste
- 2 cups frozen peas
- 1 jalapeno pepper, thinly sliced

Direction

- Soak sweetbreads in a large bowl of water for 1 hour; drain.
- Place sweetbreads in a saucepan and cover with cold water; bring to a boil. Drain. Run cold water over sweetbreads to cool.
- Return sweetbreads to the saucepan and cover with cold water again. Add 1 tablespoon butter, lemon juice, and salt; bring to a boil. Simmer for 10 minutes. Remove from heat and let cool.
- Melt 3 tablespoons butter in a heavy-bottomed skillet over medium heat. Add mushrooms; cook and stir until tender, about

5 minutes. Transfer to a plate.
- Melt remaining 3 tablespoons butter in the skillet. Add flour; cook and stir until a paste forms, about 1 minute. Season with paprika and cayenne. Pour in milk slowly, whisking until sauce is smooth, 3 to 5 minutes.
- Stir sweetbreads, mushrooms, and peas into the sauce; cook until peas are heated through, about 5 minutes. Season sweetbreads with salt. Serve garnished with jalapeno pepper.

Nutrition Information

- Calories: 375 calories
- Total Fat: 31.6 g
- Cholesterol: 326 mg
- Sodium: 242 mg
- Total Carbohydrate: 4.8 g
- Protein: 17.8 g

147. Spinach and Mushroom Frittata

"Looking for a vegetable with super health powers? Try spinach. It's packed with vitamins, minerals and antioxidants that protect you all your life."

Serving: 6

Ingredients

- 1 (10 ounce) package frozen chopped spinach, thawed and squeezed thoroughly to remove liquid
- 4 eggs or equivalent egg substitute
- 1 cup part-skim ricotta cheese
- 3/4 cup freshly grated Parmesan cheese
- 3/4 cup chopped portobello mushrooms
- 1/2 cup finely chopped scallions with some green tops
- 1/4 teaspoon dried Italian seasonings
- 1 pinch Salt and pepper, to taste

Direction

- Preheat oven to 375 degrees.
- In a large bowl, whisk together all ingredients until well mixed. Spray a 9-inch pie plate with cooking spray and fill with the spinach mixture.
- Bake for 30 minutes, or until browned and set. Let cool for 20 minutes, cut in wedges and serve.

Nutrition Information

- Calories: 167 calories
- Total Fat: 9.7 g
- Cholesterol: 146 mg
- Sodium: 288 mg
- Total Carbohydrate: 6.1 g
- Protein: 14.9 g

148. Spinach Stuffed Portobello Mushrooms

"Mix together spinach, pepperoni, and cheese for delicious easy appetizer."

Serving: 4 | Prep: 15 m | Cook: 25 m | Ready in: 40 m

Ingredients

- 4 large portobello mushroom caps, stems and gills removed
- 1 tablespoon reduced-fat Italian salad dressing
- 1 egg
- 1 clove garlic, minced
- salt and ground black pepper to taste
- 1 (10 ounce) bag fresh spinach, chopped
- 1/4 cup chopped pepperoni
- 1/4 cup grated Parmesan cheese
- 1/4 cup shredded mozzarella cheese, divided
- 3 tablespoons seasoned bread crumbs, divided

Direction

- Preheat oven to 350 degrees F (175 degrees C).
- Brush both sides of each portobello mushroom cap with Italian dressing. Arrange mushroom on a baking sheet, gill sides up.
- Bake mushrooms in the preheated oven until tender, about 12 minutes. Drain any juice that has formed in the mushrooms.
- Beat egg, garlic, salt, and black pepper together in a large bowl.
- Stir spinach, pepperoni, Parmesan cheese, 3 tablespoons mozzarella cheese, and 3 tablespoons bread crumbs into the

- eggs until evenly mixed.
- Divide spinach mixture over mushroom caps; sprinkle mushrooms with remaining 1 tablespoon mozzarella cheese and 1 tablespoon bread crumbs. Return mushrooms to the oven.
- Continue baking until topping is golden brown and cheese is melted, about 10 minutes more.

Nutrition Information

- Calories: 168 calories
- Total Fat: 10.7 g
- Cholesterol: 70 mg
- Sodium: 591 mg
- Total Carbohydrate: 7.5 g
- Protein: 11.3 g

149. Spinach Stuffed Portobello Mushrooms with Avocado

"These mushrooms are delicious on their own, or put them on toasted sourdough bread with Dijon mustard for a great veggie sandwich. Use a mixture of chopped fresh Italian herbs (oregano, basil, thyme, and parsley)."

Serving: 4 | Prep: 15 m | Cook: 15 m | Ready in: 50 m

Ingredients

- 6 sun-dried tomatoes
- 4 large portobello mushrooms, stems reserved and gills removed
- extra-virgin olive oil, or as needed
- 1 tablespoon chopped fresh oregano
- sea salt to taste
- ground black pepper to taste
- 1 large red bell pepper, cut into 1-inch pieces
- 2 cloves garlic, coarsely chopped
- 1 tablespoon extra-virgin olive oil
- 2 (10 ounce) bags fresh spinach leaves
- 3 large avocados - peeled, pitted, and diced
- 1/4 cup grated Parmesan cheese

Direction

- Soak sun-dried tomatoes in a bowl of hot water until softened, about 20 minutes. Drain.
- Preheat oven to 400 degrees F (200 degrees C).
- Line a baking sheet with parchment paper.

- Rub the caps of the portobello mushrooms with 2 tablespoons olive oil, or as needed; arrange mushrooms gill sides up on the prepared baking sheet. Season mushrooms with oregano, sea salt, and black pepper.
- Bake mushrooms in the preheated oven until tender, 8 to 10 minutes.
- Place the mushroom stems, sun-dried tomatoes, red bell pepper, and garlic cloves in a food processor; pulse until finely chopped.
- Heat 1 tablespoon olive oil in a large skillet over medium-high heat. Cook and stir sun-dried tomato mixture in the hot oil until fragrant, about 2 minutes.
- Stir spinach into the skillet; cover, reduce heat to medium-low, and cook until spinach is wilted, about 3 minutes more, stirring occasionally. Drain excess liquid from skillet.
- Spoon spinach mixture over baked mushroom caps.
- Divide diced avocado atop stuff mushrooms and sprinkle with Parmesan cheese to serve.

Nutrition Information

- Calories: 539 calories
- Total Fat: 43.8 g
- Cholesterol: 4 mg
- Sodium: 364 mg
- Total Carbohydrate: 34.1 g
- Protein: 14 g

150. Stuffed Portobello Mushrooms

"Stuffed with pork sausage, shredded and ricotta cheeses, onions and sun-dried tomatoes, these tasty mushroom caps are a sure crowd pleaser."

Serving: 12 | Prep: 20 m | Cook: 10 m | Ready in: 30 m

Ingredients

- 1 (9.6 ounce) package Jimmy Dean® Original Hearty Pork Sausage Crumbles
- 2 cups shredded Italian cheese blend, divided
- 1/2 cup ricotta cheese
- 2 green onions, thinly sliced
- 3 tablespoons finely chopped sun-dried tomatoes, rehydrated
- 12 medium portobello mushroom caps
- 2 tablespoons olive oil
- 3 tablespoons balsamic vinegar (optional)

Direction

- Preheat oven to 350 degrees F. Combine sausage, 1 cup shredded cheese, ricotta cheese, onions and tomatoes in large bowl.
- Brush tops of mushroom caps with oil; place, top-sides down, in shallow baking pan.
- Top with sausage mixture. Drizzle with vinegar, if desired. Sprinkle with remaining shredded cheese.
- Bake 10-12 minutes or until mushrooms are tender.

Nutrition Information

- Calories: 202 calories
- Total Fat: 14.9 g
- Cholesterol: 30 mg
- Sodium: 287 mg
- Total Carbohydrate: 8.2 g
- Protein: 10.7 g

151. Summer Vegetarian Chili

"Throw summer's fresh vegetables into a pot and stew them up for an antioxidant-packed, Southwestern-flavored treat. Black beans also have fiber, folic acid and cholesterol-lowering activity."

Serving: 6

Ingredients

- 2 tablespoons extra-virgin olive oil
- 1 cup chopped red onion
- 5 large cloves garlic, crushed or minced
- 2 tablespoons chili powder, or more to taste
- 2 teaspoons ground cumin
- 2 cups juicy chopped fresh tomatoes
- 1 (15 ounce) can no-salt-added black beans, drained
- 1 cup water (or red wine)
- 1 cup chopped bell pepper (any color)
- 1 cup chopped zucchini
- 1 cup corn kernels
- 1 cup chopped white or portobello mushrooms
- 1 cup chopped fresh cilantro, packed
- 1/8 teaspoon cayenne pepper, or more to taste
- Salt and freshly ground black pepper, to taste

Direction

- Heat oil in medium pot. Add onion, garlic, chili powder and cumin. Sauté over medium heat until onion is soft, about 5 minutes. Add remaining ingredients (except garnishes) and stir.

Bring to a boil, then lower heat and simmer 20 minutes or until vegetables are soft. Add more liquid if needed.
- Serve alone or over rice (preferably brown). Garnish if desired with any of the following: reduced-fat cheddar cheese, onion, fat-free sour cream, guacamole, fresh cilantro.

Nutrition Information

- Calories: 178 calories
- Total Fat: 5.8 g
- Cholesterol: 0 mg
- Sodium: 640 mg
- Total Carbohydrate: 27.8 g
- Protein: 7.1 g

152. Swedish Turkey Meatballs with Cream of Mushroom Soup

"After searching high and low for a nummy ground turkey Swedish meatballs recipe all 4 kiddos and the husband would love, I decided to just come up with my own using ground turkey and lots of creamy mushroom soup sauce."

Serving: 12 | Prep: 20 m | Cook: 1 h | Ready in: 1 h 20 m

Ingredients

- Meatballs:
- 2 teaspoons vegetable oil, or as needed
- 1/2 cup milk
- 2 eggs
- 1 1/2 pounds ground turkey, or more to taste
- 1 cup crushed chicken-flavored crackers (such as Nabisco® Chicken in a Biscuit)
- 1/2 onion, minced
- 1 teaspoon salt
- 1 teaspoon ground nutmeg
- 1 teaspoon ground black pepper
- Sauce:
- 2 (10.75 ounce) cans cream of mushroom soup
- 2 (10.75 ounce) cans condensed golden mushroom soup
- 1 (12 fluid ounce) can evaporated milk
- 1 (8 ounce) carton sour cream
- 1/2 pound baby portobello mushrooms, sliced
- 2 cloves garlic, minced
- 1 cup grated Parmesan cheese
- 1 (16 ounce) package egg noodles

Direction

- Preheat the oven to 350 degrees F (175 degrees C). Lightly oil a baking sheet and a 2-quart casserole dish.
- Whisk milk and eggs together in a bowl. Add turkey, crackers, onion, salt, nutmeg, and black pepper. Mix well. Shape into 1-inch balls and place on the prepared baking sheet.
- Bake in the preheated oven until browned, about 20 minutes. Drain meatballs on paper towels and transfer to the prepared casserole dish. Leave oven on.
- Combine cream of mushroom soup, golden mushroom soup, evaporated milk, sour cream, mushrooms, and garlic in a large bowl; stir until smooth. Pour over the meatballs in the casserole dish.
- Bake in the hot oven until bubbling, about 40 minutes.
- Bring a large pot of lightly salted water to a boil. Cook egg noodles in the boiling water, stirring occasionally, until tender yet firm to the bite, about 8 minutes. Drain. Serve meatballs and gravy over hot noodles; sprinkle with Parmesan cheese before serving.

Nutrition Information

- Calories: 500 calories
- Total Fat: 23.4 g
- Cholesterol: 130 mg
- Sodium: 1171 mg
- Total Carbohydrate: 46.5 g
- Protein: 26.1 g

153. Teresas Hearty Chicken Cacciatore

"The secret ingredient which makes this cacciatore stand out is pancetta, an Italian bacon. Once a specialty deli item, it is now readily available at most major supermarkets. The pancetta gives the sauce richness and body. I've also found that fresh basil leaves and baby portobello mushrooms make it my own. It is kid-friendly and fills the house with a wonderful aroma."

Serving: 6 | Prep: 25 m | Cook: 50 m | Ready in: 1 h 15 m

Ingredients

- extra virgin olive oil
- 1/4 pound pancetta (Italian bacon), thickly sliced
- 1/2 cup all-purpose flour
- 1 tablespoon dried Italian herb seasoning
- 1 tablespoon red pepper flakes
- 6 chicken thighs with skin and bone
- 1 small green bell pepper, chopped
- 1 small sweet onion, diced
- 1 pound baby portobello mushrooms, sliced
- 1/2 cup chopped fresh basil
- 3 cloves garlic, chopped
- 3 tablespoons tomato paste
- 1 (28 ounce) can diced tomatoes with juice
- 1/2 cup dry red wine, or more to taste
- 1 tablespoon cornstarch (optional)
- 2 tablespoons water (optional)
- 1 (16 ounce) package rigatoni pasta
- freshly shredded Parmesan cheese to taste
- salt and ground black pepper to taste

Direction

- Heat the olive oil in a large nonstick skillet over medium heat, and cook and stir the pancetta until it begins to turn dark brown, 5 to 8 minutes. Remove the pancetta pieces from the skillet with a slotted spoon and set aside.
- Mix the flour, Italian seasoning, and red pepper flakes in a shallow bowl.
- Press the chicken thighs into the flour mixture, tapping off any loose flour.
- Brown the chicken thighs in the skillet with the oil and pancetta drippings, 8 to 10 minutes per side. Transfer the chicken thighs to a platter and keep warm.
- Cook and stir the green bell pepper, sweet onion, and portobello mushrooms in the same skillet until the onion turns translucent, about 8 minutes.
- Stir the basil, garlic, tomato paste, diced tomatoes with their juice, and red wine into the sauce.
- Bring the sauce to a boil, and return the chicken and pancetta to the sauce. If sauce does not almost cover the chicken pieces, mix in more dry red wine.
- Reduce heat to low, and simmer the chicken and sauce until the chicken thighs are tender and no longer pink inside, 35 to 50 minutes.
- If you prefer a thicker sauce, whisk cornstarch with water and 1 tablespoon of the sauce, and stir the mixture into the skillet until thickened.
- About 15 minutes before serving time, bring a large pot of lightly salted water and bring to a boil.
- Stir in the rigatoni and return to a boil. Cook uncovered over medium heat, stirring occasionally, until the pasta has cooked through but is still slightly firm, about 13 minutes; drain.

- To serve, transfer the cooked rigatoni to a large platter and top with the chicken thighs.
- Generously ladle sauce over the chicken and pasta, and sprinkle the dish with Parmesan cheese, salt, and black pepper. Serve any extra sauce on the side.

Nutrition Information

- Calories: 654 calories
- Total Fat: 21.1 g
- Cholesterol: 72 mg
- Sodium: 505 mg
- Total Carbohydrate: 77.1 g
- Protein: 35.6 g

154. Tofu and Portobello Mushroom Parmigiana

"Breaded tofu and portobello a la Parmigiana. Great meal that builds on the original recipe. The portobello mushrooms add nice flavor and texture to the meal."

Serving: 4 | Prep: 30 m | Cook: 25 m | Ready in: 55 m

Ingredients

- 1 cup seasoned bread crumbs
- 1/2 cup grated Parmesan cheese, divided
- 4 teaspoons dried oregano, divided
- salt and ground black pepper to taste
- 1 (12 ounce) package firm tofu, cut into four 1/4-inch thick slices
- 4 portobello mushrooms, stems removed
- 1/4 cup olive oil, divided
- 1 (8 ounce) can tomato sauce
- 2 cloves garlic, minced
- 1/2 teaspoon dried basil
- 6 ounces shredded mozzarella cheese

Direction

- Preheat oven to 400 degrees F (200 degrees C).
- Stir bread crumbs, 3 tablespoons Parmesan cheese, 2 teaspoons oregano, salt, and black pepper together in a bowl.
- Place tofu in a bowl of cold water. Place mushrooms in a separate bowl of cold water. Remove 1 mushroom from water; press mushroom into bread crumb mixture and turn to coat all

sides. Transfer breaded mushroom to a plate. Repeat with remaining mushrooms and tofu slices.
- Heat 2 tablespoons olive oil in a skillet over medium heat. Cook breaded tofu and mushrooms in hot oil until browned on one side, 2 to 3 minutes. Drizzle a little olive oil over the top, turn mushrooms and tofu slices, and cook until browned on the other side, about 2 minutes more.
- Whisk tomato sauce, garlic, remaining oregano, and basil together in a bowl until sauce is smooth. Spread a thin layer of sauce into the bottom of an 8-inch square baking dish. Arrange tofu slices in a single layer over sauce, and top each tofu slice with a mushroom. Spoon remaining sauce over mushrooms and tofu; top with mozzarella cheese and remaining Parmesan cheese.
- Bake in the preheated oven until cheese melts and mixture is bubbling, about 20 minutes.

Nutrition Information

- Calories: 559 calories
- Total Fat: 32.7 g
- Cholesterol: 36 mg
- Sodium: 1295 mg
- Total Carbohydrate: 36 g
- Protein: 35.7 g

155. Turkey Mushroom Gravy

"I have been making Thanksgiving dinner every year since the 1970's. I have tried every kind of turkey gravy. I created this recipe about 15 years ago. It is everyone's favorite, even the people who hate mushrooms. Serve with roasted turkey and cornbread stuffing!"

Serving: 20 | Prep: 30 m | Cook: 2 h | Ready in: 2 h 30 m

Ingredients

- 2 cups unsalted butter
- 1 pound portobello mushrooms, wiped clean with paper towels
- 2 pounds whole white mushrooms, wiped clean with paper towels
- 1 cup all-purpose flour
- 4 (14.5 ounce) cans chicken broth
- 1 1/2 cups turkey pan drippings
- 2 cups chopped onions
- 1 cup chopped celery
- salt and pepper to taste
- 1/4 teaspoon cayenne pepper

Direction

- Melt butter in a large stock pot over medium-low heat, and cook the mushrooms until they are browned and the butter is clear, 1 to 1 1/2 hours. Remove the mushrooms, coarsely chop them, and set aside. There should be about 1 cup of butter left in the stock pot; whisk the flour into the butter, and gently cook over low heat until the flour mixture turns mahogany brown in color,

about 20 minutes. Whisk in the chicken broth; bring the mixture to a simmer to thicken the stock.
- Pour the turkey drippings into a saucepan, then cook and stir the onions and celery in the drippings over medium-low heat until the onions begin to turn brown, about 20 minutes. Stir the drippings and vegetables into the thickened stock. Bring the gravy to a gentle boil, reduce heat, and simmer for about 20 minutes to blend the flavors. Stir in the chopped mushrooms, then season to taste with salt, black pepper, and cayenne pepper.

Nutrition Information

- Calories: 347 calories
- Total Fat: 34 g
- Cholesterol: 64 mg
- Sodium: 12 mg
- Total Carbohydrate: 9.1 g
- Protein: 3 g

156. Turkey Portobello Pizza

"This delicious mushroom pizza is easy and fun. You can substitute the turkey meat to make it vegetarian, too!"

Serving: 4 | Prep: 20 m | Cook: 25 m | Ready in: 45 m

Ingredients

- 4 large portobello mushroom caps, stems removed
- 1/4 cup extra-virgin olive oil
- 3 tablespoons extra-virgin olive oil
- 1 small red onion, diced
- 2 cloves garlic, minced
- 1 pound ground turkey
- salt to taste
- 2 roma (plum) tomatoes, diced
- 1 (8 ounce) jar basil pesto
- 6 ounces fresh mozzarella cheese, sliced
- 2 ounces grated Parmesan cheese

Direction

- Preheat oven to 350 degrees F (175 degrees C).
- Lightly grease a baking sheet.
- Coat portobello mushrooms with about 1/4 cup olive oil on both sides; arrange mushrooms gill-side up on a baking sheet.
- Heat 3 tablespoons olive oil in a large skillet over high heat. Cook and stir onion and garlic in hot oil until onion begins to turn translucent, 3 to 5 minutes.
- Stir turkey into onion mixture and reduce heat to medium-high; season with salt. Continue cooking and stirring until turkey is no

longer pink, 5 to 7 minutes.
- Drain turkey, reserving about 1 tablespoon grease in the skillet.
- Stir tomatoes and pesto sauce into the turkey; simmer, stirring occasionally, until the sauce is heated through, 5 to 7 minutes.
- Place a slice of mozzarella cheese in the center of each mushroom cap and sprinkle evenly with Parmesan cheese.
- Divide turkey pesto sauce evenly over the mushroom caps.
- Bake in the preheated oven until cheese has melted, 10 to 15 minutes.

Nutrition Information

- Calories: 871 calories
- Total Fat: 71.3 g
- Cholesterol: 143 mg
- Sodium: 1012 mg
- Total Carbohydrate: 9.1 g
- Protein: 49.7 g

157. Vegan Portobello Stroganoff

"A vegan version of an old classic. Meaty marinated portobellos give this dish the taste and mouth-feel of the original."

Serving: 4 | Prep: 10 m | Cook: 40 m | Ready in: 1 h 10 m

Ingredients

- 8 ounces vegan sour cream (such as Tofutti®)
- 1/2 cup water
- 3 tablespoons dried minced onion
- 2 tablespoons all-purpose flour
- 2 teaspoons vegan no-beef bouillon
- 1/4 teaspoon garlic powder
- 1/4 teaspoon dried basil
- 1/4 teaspoon ground black pepper
- 1/2 cup dry red wine
- 1 tablespoon olive oil
- 2 tablespoons soy sauce
- 1 tablespoon balsamic vinegar
- 2 cloves garlic, minced
- 2 large portobello mushroom caps, stems and gills removed
- cooking spray
- 1/4 cup water, or as needed (optional)

Direction

- Whisk vegan sour cream, 1/2 cup water, minced onion, flour, vegan bouillon, garlic powder, basil, and black pepper in a bowl. Cover and refrigerate.
- Preheat oven to 400 degrees F (200 degrees C).

- Whisk red wine, olive oil, soy sauce, balsamic vinegar, and garlic in another bowl.
- Arrange mushroom caps with gill sides up in a baking dish and pour red wine mixture on top. Marinate for 20 minutes, then cover baking dish with aluminum foil.
- Bake mushrooms in the preheated oven for 30 minutes. Remove foil, flip mushrooms, and continue baking until very tender, about 10 minutes more. Set aside to cool; dice mushrooms.
- Heat a saucepan sprayed with cooking spray over medium heat. Cook and stir mushrooms in sauce pan until lightly browned, about 5 minutes; reduce heat to low.
- Stir sour cream sauce into mushrooms. Continue to cook and stir until thickened, 1 to 2 minutes more. If the sauce becomes too thick, stir in 1/4 cup water.

Nutrition Information

- Calories: 259 calories
- Total Fat: 13.5 g
- Cholesterol: 0 mg
- Sodium: 778 mg
- Total Carbohydrate: 25.9 g
- Protein: 3.3 g

158. Vegan Spaghetti

"Super tasty, low-fat vegan spaghetti is a celiac-friendly Italian dish."

Serving: 1 | Prep: 20 m | Cook: 20 m | Ready in: 40 m

Ingredients

- 1 large zucchini
- 1/2 cup vegetable broth, or as needed, divided
- 1 small onion, diced
- 1 1/2 tablespoons tomato paste
- 1 small tomato, diced
- 1 small portobello mushroom, cubed
- 1 tablespoon minced garlic
- 2 teaspoons dried oregano
- 1 teaspoon dried thyme
- 1/2 teaspoon dried tarragon
- 1/2 teaspoon dried marjoram
- 1/2 (12 ounce) package veggie meat substitute (such as Yves® Ground Round)
- 2 cups fresh spinach, roughly chopped

Direction

- Cut zucchini into noodles using a spiralizer fitted with the large shredding blade. Set aside.
- Combine 1/4 cup broth, onion, and tomato paste in a large saucepan over medium heat. Cook until onion begins to soften, about 3 minutes. Add tomato, mushroom, garlic, oregano, thyme, tarragon, and marjoram. Cook until the mushroom just begins to soften, about 3 minutes more.

- Stir veggie meat, spinach, and remaining 1/4 cup broth into the pan with the mushroom mixture. Add an additional 1/4 cup broth if the pan seems dry. Cook and stir until vegetables are tender and sauce is beginning to thicken, about 10 minutes.
- Stir zucchini noodles into the pan with the sauce and cook to desired firmness, 3 to 5 minutes more.

Nutrition Information

- Calories: 442 calories
- Total Fat: 9.9 g
- Cholesterol: 0 mg
- Sodium: 1189 mg
- Total Carbohydrate: 53 g
- Protein: 43.1 g

159. VegetableStuffed Portobello Mushrooms

"This is the perfect way to eat your vegetables and add another recipe to your list of vegetarian meals. The dish can be served alone or over angel hair pasta. Any leftover stuffing can be used the next day in an egg white omelet."

Serving: 4 | Prep: 25 m | Cook: 12 m | Ready in: 1 h 37 m

Ingredients

- 1 cup balsamic vinegar
- 1/2 teaspoon garlic powder
- 1/2 teaspoon onion powder
- 4 large portobello mushrooms, wiped clean and stems removed
- 2 tablespoons olive oil
- 1 small eggplant, peeled and diced
- 1 cup frozen spinach
- 1/2 cup shredded mozzarella cheese
- 2 plum tomatoes, diced
- 1 (6 ounce) jar artichoke hearts in brine, drained and chopped
- 1/4 cup grated Parmesan cheese

Direction

- Stir the balsamic vinegar, garlic powder, and onion powder together in a small bowl until blended. Place the mushrooms into a large resealable plastic bag. Pour in the balsamic vinegar mixture, seal bag, and turn gently to coat mushrooms evenly with marinade. Place in refrigerator for 1 hour.
- Place the olive oil into a skillet, and heat over medium-high heat. Stir in the eggplant and spinach; cook and stir until

eggplant turns golden brown, about 5 minutes.
- Preheat oven to 350 degrees F (175 degrees C). Lightly grease 9x13 inch baking dish.
- Remove mushrooms from marinade, shake off any excess, and discard marinade. Place mushrooms in prepared dish, top side down. Spoon the eggplant and spinach mixture evenly over the mushrooms. Sprinkle with mozzarella cheese. Divide the tomatoes and artichoke hearts evenly between the mushrooms. Top each mushroom with Parmesan cheese.
- Place in preheated oven, and bake until the cheese melts, about 12 minutes. Serve hot.

Nutrition Information

- Calories: 260 calories
- Total Fat: 11.7 g
- Cholesterol: 15 mg
- Sodium: 495 mg
- Total Carbohydrate: 29.9 g
- Protein: 13.4 g

160. Vegetarian MushroomWalnut Meatloaf

"This is a different and delicious veggie meatloaf that's a nice diversion from the basic soy protein based veggie meatloaf recipes out there."

Serving: 6 | Prep: 45 m | Cook: 1 h | Ready in: 1 h 55 m

Ingredients

- 1 tablespoon olive oil
- 12 ounces crimini mushrooms, chopped
- 1 small red onion, finely diced
- 1 red bell pepper, seeded and diced
- 1 tablespoon ground sage
- 1 1/4 cups cooked brown rice
- 1/2 cup walnuts, finely chopped
- 1 envelope onion soup mix
- 1 cup oat bran
- 1 cup wheat germ
- 2 egg whites, lightly beaten
- 1 teaspoon Worcestershire sauce
- 2 teaspoons prepared mustard

Direction

- Preheat oven to 350 degrees F (175 degrees C). Lightly grease a 9x5 inch loaf pan.
- Heat the olive oil in a large skillet over medium heat. Stir in the mushrooms, onions, and bell pepper; cook until the onion is transparent, about 5 minutes. Sprinkle sage over the

vegetables, and cook until vegetables are soft, about 5 minutes more. Transfer vegetables to a large mixing bowl.
- Stir the rice, walnuts, onion soup mix, oat bran, wheat germ, egg whites, Worcestershire sauce, and mustard into the mushroom mixture until thoroughly blended. Spoon into prepared loaf pan, pressing down mixture with a spatula to flatten top.
- Bake in preheated oven for 1 hour. Let rest 10 minutes before slicing.

Nutrition Information

- Calories: 384 calories
- Total Fat: 12.8 g
- Cholesterol: 0 mg
- Sodium: 468 mg
- Total Carbohydrate: 59.3 g
- Protein: 16 g

161. Wilted Arugula and Portobello Mushrooms

"Arugula and portobello mushrooms are simmered with onion, garlic, sherry, and red pepper flakes. A tasty side dish and good way to get some veggies! You can easily substitute wine for the sherry and veggie broth for the chicken broth depending on your preferences."

Serving: 2 | Prep: 20 m | Cook: 10 m | Ready in: 30 m

Ingredients

- 1 tablespoon olive oil
- 1/2 small onion, chopped
- 2 cloves garlic, minced
- 1/8 teaspoon crushed red pepper flakes, or to taste
- 1 portobello mushroom cap, chopped
- 1/4 cup dry sherry
- 1/4 cup chicken broth
- 4 cups arugula leaves
- 1/8 teaspoon ground black pepper

Direction

- Heat olive oil in a large skillet over medium heat. Add onion and garlic and cook until soft, about 5 minutes. Stir in red pepper flakes and chopped mushrooms and cook until mushrooms are coated with oil and begin to soften.
- Pour in sherry and chicken broth. Simmer until liquid is reduced by half. Add arugula and cook until wilted, about one minute. Season with black pepper. Serve immediately.

Nutrition Information

- Calories: 125 calories
- Total Fat: 7.2 g
- Cholesterol: 0 mg
- Sodium: 195 mg
- Total Carbohydrate: 11.8 g
- Protein: 2.9 g

162. Winter Minestra

"This beef-based minestra is great for cold winter days. Serve in individual bowls with Parmesan cheese and parsley sprinkled over the top."

Serving: 10 | Prep: 20 m | Cook: 25 m | Ready in: 45 m

Ingredients

- 1 pound ground beef
- 1 tablespoon olive oil
- 2 cloves garlic, chopped
- 1 onion, chopped
- 1 head cauliflower, chopped
- 2 jalapeno peppers, seeded and chopped
- 1 shallot, finely chopped
- 2 portobello mushrooms, diced
- salt and pepper to taste
- 2 (14.5 ounce) cans stewed tomatoes
- 4 cups beef broth
- 1 pinch crushed red pepper flakes
- 1 (10 ounce) package frozen mixed vegetables, thawed

Direction

- Crumble the ground beef into a large stockpot set over medium heat. Cook and stir until meat is no longer pink. Drain off excess grease and add the olive oil. Heat the oil and add the garlic and onion; cook and stir until the onion is tender. Add cauliflower, jalapenos, shallot and mushrooms. Season with salt and cook for 8 to 10 minutes to release the water from the vegetables.

- Pour in the stewed tomatoes and season with red pepper flakes. Stir aggressively to break up the tomatoes. Pour in the beef broth and mixed vegetables and bring to a simmer. Cook until frozen vegetables are tender. Taste and adjust salt and pepper before serving.

Nutrition Information

- Calories: 169 calories
- Total Fat: 7.3 g
- Cholesterol: 28 mg
- Sodium: 554 mg
- Total Carbohydrate: 15.4 g
- Protein: 12.4 g

Chapter 2: Enoki
***

163. ABC Ribeye Steak

"Got some good steaks in the fridge, but the weather isn't cooperating with your grilling plans? Try stir-frying your steaks in this Chinese-inspired dish with mixed Asian ingredients. Quick and easy, always a hit!"

Serving: 4 | Prep: 25 m | Cook: 10 m | Ready in: 35 m

Ingredients

- Sauce:
- 3 tablespoons oyster sauce
- 2 tablespoons soy sauce
- 1 tablespoon mirin (sweetened rice wine)
- 2 tablespoons olive oil, divided
- 1 large red onion, halved and thinly sliced
- 2 (10 ounce) ribeye steaks, sliced 1/4-inch thick and 1-inch long
- 8 heads baby bok choy, trimmed
- 1/3 (12 ounce) package tofu, cut into 1/3-inch cubes
- 1 (3 ounce) package enoki mushrooms, roots removed

Direction

- Mix oyster sauce, soy sauce, and mirin together in a small bowl to make sauce.
- Heat 1 tablespoon oil in a wok or large skillet over high heat until shimmering, about 1 minute. Add red onion; cook and stir until golden, about 1 minute. Transfer to a plate.
- Heat remaining 1 tablespoon oil in the same wok over high heat. Add steak; sauté to desired doneness, 3 to 5 minutes. Transfer to a plate, reserving juices in the wok.

- Return onion to the wok. Stir in bok choy, tofu, and enoki mushrooms. Cook and stir until tofu is heated through and bok choy is wilted, about 3 minutes. Return steak to the wok. Stir in sauce, tossing to coat.

Nutrition Information

- Calories: 421 calories
- Total Fat: 23.1 g
- Cholesterol: 50 mg
- Sodium: 1167 mg
- Total Carbohydrate: 27.5 g
- Protein: 32.8 g

164. Asian Chicken and Corn Soup

"This soup recipe is great for cold winter nights, or as a starter for an Asian meal. None of the ingredients are hard to find, and the result is warming and delicious!"

Serving: 6 | Prep: 25 m | Cook: 30 m | Ready in: 55 m

Ingredients

- 1 tablespoon vegetable oil
- 10 button mushrooms, sliced thin
- 10 small oyster mushrooms, sliced thin
- 1 (3 ounce) package enoki mushrooms, roots removed
- 1/4 cup chopped onion
- 1/4 cup chopped celery
- 1/4 cup chopped green bell pepper
- 1/4 cup chopped carrot
- 3 cloves garlic, smashed
- salt and pepper to taste
- 2 (14.5 ounce) cans chicken broth
- 1 (15 ounce) can cream-style corn
- 1 (5 ounce) can chunk white chicken (such as Swanson®), drained
- 1 tablespoon rice wine vinegar
- 2 teaspoons Chinese five-spice powder
- 1 tablespoon cornstarch
- 1/2 cup cold milk
- 15 leaves fresh Thai basil, chopped

Direction

- Heat the vegetable oil in a large pot over medium-high heat. Stir in the button mushrooms, oyster mushrooms, and enoki mushrooms; cook and stir until lightly browned. Add the onion, celery, green bell pepper, carrot, and garlic. Season with salt and pepper. Cook and stir for 3 to 4 minutes. Mix in the chicken broth, cream-style corn, chicken, rice wine vinegar, and five-spice powder, and bring to boil. Cover and reduce heat to medium-low. Simmer for about 20 minutes. Mix cornstarch with the milk in a small bowl, and stir into the soup. Stir until soup has thickened. Garnish each serving with chopped basil.

Nutrition Information

- Calories: 168 calories
- Total Fat: 5.3 g
- Cholesterol: 16 mg
- Sodium: 371 mg
- Total Carbohydrate: 23.2 g
- Protein: 9.7 g

165. Bacon Wrapped Delights

"You can wrap almost anything in bacon and it'll taste great. Here is a recipe that works great as appetizers or as hors d'oeuvres. This dish can be served plain or accompanied with a hollandaise sauce or orange ponzu sauce."

Serving: 6 | Prep: 25 m | Cook: 15 m | Ready in: 40 m

Ingredients

- 12 spears white asparagus
- 4 ounces enoki mushrooms
- 4 ounces shiitake mushrooms, stemmed and sliced 1/4-inch thick
- 24 slices bacon

Direction

- Preheat oven to 425 degrees F (220 degrees C).
- Bring a pot of water to a boil. Blanch the asparagus until it is barely cooked and still crisp, 2 to 4 minutes. When done, plunge the asparagus into ice water to stop the cooking. When cool, trim the asparagus to 8-inch lengths. Wrap a bundle of 6 asparagus spears with six strips of bacon, side by side, securing each slice with a toothpick. The bacon should be wrapped around twice so that there are two layers.
- Trim the enoki mushrooms, and separate into 12 pieces. Stuff each enoki piece with four pieces of shiitake. Wrap each bundle with a slice of bacon, wrapping around twice, and secure with a toothpick. Place the bundles on a wire rack placed over a baking sheet.

- Roast in preheated oven for 6 minutes, then flip the bundles over, and cook for another 4 to 6 minutes, until the bacon is brown and crisp.
- To serve, remove all 24 toothpicks, and slice the asparagus bundles between the bacon. Drain on paper towels for a moment before serving.

Nutrition Information

- Calories: 225 calories
- Total Fat: 15.6 g
- Cholesterol: 41 mg
- Sodium: 859 mg
- Total Carbohydrate: 4.9 g
- Protein: 15.6 g

Printed in Great Britain
by Amazon